**If you want the old battalion,
We know where they are
– Hanging on the old barbed wire**

A Barbed Wire Book

First published in 1999 by Barbed Wire, PO Box 958, London W14 OJF

Printed by The Russell Press Ltd, Russell House, Bulwell Lane, Basford, Nottingham NG6 0BT

This book was produced by ex-soldiers. The text was compiled and written by Aly Renwick who served eight years in the British Army in the 1960s.

While responsibility for the contents rests with Aly Renwick, he would like to thank the following for providing information or giving advice and criticism: Peter and Dorothy Berresford Ellis, Chris Reeves, Margaret Henry and Caleb Henry-Smith, Chris Tranchell, Micheál Mac Donncha, Bill Rolston, Clara Reilly and friends, Kirsty Malcolm, Orlee Udwin, Susan Schonfield, Tim O'Grady, Mitzy Carlough, Oliver Donohue, Martin Collins and Elizabeth Kearney.

Nina Hutchison and Joan Maynard both gave me encouragement – their deaths saddened all who knew them, they are greatly missed.

I would especially like to thank Paul Donovan, Pat Harper, John Lloyd, Frances Mary Blake and Liz Curtis for their aid and support, and Adrian Yeeles for his help with the design.

Thanks also to the Vietnam Veterans in Chicago and Detroit who warmly welcomed me and provided information and solidarity. Among the Northern Ireland veterans who provided knowledge and assistance at different times over three decades were: Brian Ashton, Mike Biggs, Chris Byrne, Lloyd Hayes, Dave Swingler, Meurig Parri, Duncan Melville, Bobby Harker, Alan Robe, Dave Roach, Lou McGrath and Alex Hardman. The veterans in jail who alerted me to the many ex-soldiers in British prisons were: Shaun Gorman, John James Claxton and Jimmy Johnson who deserves a special mention as he was the inspiration for *Hidden Wounds*. From his prison cell Jimmy continues to fight for recognition that he and many other veterans are suffering from post-traumatic stress disorder.

British Library Cataloguing in Publication Data
A catalogue record for this book is available from the British Library

ISBN 0 9533833 0 X

Trade distribution by Turnaround Publisher Services
Unit 3, Olympia Trading Estate, Coburg Road,
London N22 6TZ
Tel: 0181 829 3000
Fax: 0181 881 5088

They ask me where I've been,
And what I've done and seen.
But what can I reply
Who knows it wasn't I,
But someone just like me,
Who went across the sea
And with my head and hands
Killed men in foreign lands ...
Though I must bear the blame,
Because he bore my name.

**'Back', by Wilfred Gibson,
a First World War veteran**

'They gave me a Bronze Star ... and they put me up for a Silver Star. But I said you can shove it up your ass. ... I threw all the others away. The only thing I kept was the Purple Heart because I still think I was wounded.'
A Vietnam veteran

'Christ, I remember the day we arrived in Ulster. All the Rambos in our regiment [1st Battalion Royal Regiment of Fusiliers] were loving it – they were crazy – they thought this was all some film, like. I knew it was no film. For every single moment I was there, for two whole bloody years, I was terrified, man, sheer terrified! Even today, man, when I hear a click, my ass hits the floor! I lost four of my best mates there, blown to bits, and I wonder now just what the hell it was all for. No, man, I have no fears in the ring, absolutely none at all. After two years crawling around Tyrone and South Armagh, it don't frighten me none!'
**Boxer Nigel Benn,
a Northern Ireland veteran**

Introduction

The early years of the conflict in Northern Ireland coincided with the latter years of the Vietnam War. One legacy of the USA's involvement in Vietnam was the psychological problems that afflicted many of the GIs after they returned home. In 1990, fifteen years after the ending of the Vietnam War, a study in the USA found that over fifteen per cent of Vietnam veterans were still suffering from post-traumatic stress disorder (PTSD). Many with this condition were unemployed and liable to abuse alcohol or drugs. Seventy per cent had failed marriages and almost half had served terms in prison.

Since 1969 many thousands of young soldiers from Britain have served tours of duty in Northern Ireland and faced varying degrees of hostility and experienced violent confrontations. While the scale of the conflict was undoubtedly greater in Vietnam, there is increasing evidence that a significant number of ex-soldiers who served in Northern Ireland have experienced rehabilitation difficulties, which parallel those of the Vietnam veterans. A study by CRISIS into homeless people in London found that 'Around one quarter of all single homeless people have served in the forces.' Twenty-nine per cent of the ex-service people interviewed said they were suffering from nerves, depression and stress. Forty-one per cent of them had spent time in prison.

Jimmy Johnson was a corporal in the Royal Tank Regiment and served two tours of duty in Northern Ireland in the early 70s. He was 'mentioned in dispatches' for rescuing a badly wounded woman civilian from a bombed building. After leaving the army Johnson killed two people and is now a category 'A' prisoner serving a life sentence in Frankland maximum security prison near Durham. Johnson believes the murders he committed as a civilian were the direct result of PTSD and he has fought a long battle from his prison cell not just for

his own case to be heard, but for all the hundreds of other ex-soldiers in prison like him.

The MoD and successive British governments have turned a blind eye to the plight of their Northern Ireland veterans and offered little help to those ex-soldiers who are having difficulty settling back into Civvy Street. *Hidden Wounds* tells the story of Jimmy Johnson and other Northern Ireland veterans, outlines the history of soldiers with PTSD and demands that the British authorities take account of the fact that many of the young soldiers who swore their allegiance to the Queen and served tours of duty in Northern Ireland with British Army Regiments have ended up serving time in Her Majesty's prisons.

Soldier Tales

On 10th July 1976, four mercenaries were executed by a military firing squad in Angola. Three of the men, Costos Georgiou, Derek 'Brummie' Barker and Andy McKenzie were former members of the British Army's Parachute Regiment and veterans of the conflict in Northern Ireland. The fourth man, Daniel Gearhart, was a US ex-Special Forces Vietnam veteran. The most infamous man to die, Georgiou, was known as 'Colonel Callan'. A BBC Panorama programme on the mercenaries said, 'In Angola it was the psychopathic exploits of the mercenary leader, the self-styled Colonel Callan, that caused public outrage. Callan, a dishonourably discharged paratrooper, ordered the execution of twelve mercenaries ... when they refused to fight.'[1] During the trial, it became clear that Georgiou had been responsible for untold deaths, both on his own side and that of the 'enemy'.

Costos Georgiou came from a family in the large Greek Cypriot community in north London. Until he joined the British army he had been described as a 'quiet, introspective youth':

> Once in the Army however, a more aggressive side to his character
> emerged. He seemed determined to prove himself the best soldier in the
> entire British Army. And, for a time, he came close to achieving his ambition:
> during training at Aldershot, he picked up awards as best machine-gunner,
> best Self-Loading Rifle-shot and best all-round recruit in the camp.

> Not content with this, he became a fitness fanatic, soon excelling at the
> physical side of army training. He went out of his way to develop a tougher,
> more aggressive image than anyone else in his unit. He spent hours in front
> of a mirror, perfecting the toughest, meanest scowl he could devise. When
> off duty he adopted a solid, swaggering walk that John Wayne might have
> been proud of.

> Such stunts were crude but they paid off – his officers took notice of him.

Of all the men in his regiment, Georgiou was the one chosen for the prestigious position of bodyguard to his Commanding Officer in Northern Ireland.[2]

One of the initiation tests for the Paras is called 'milling'. In it recruits fight each other for a set period: win or lose, they are expected to show sustained pugnacity and will be rejected by this elite unit unless they do so. This aggressive attitude, which is exacerbated during training, is instilled for conventional warfare, in which the Paras are often expected to attack and take specific targets – ahead of the main army – and hold them till other units can get there. In those circumstances, the fighting is all-out and no quarter is expected or given, and no prisoners are taken. Consequently, a para's training is tough and brutal and those who complete it are contemptuous even of other soldiers, whom they call 'craphats'.

The Parachute Regiment carried out the Bloody Sunday killings in Derry in early 1972, which left 14 civil rights demonstrators dead. Throughout Northern Ireland they have earned a notorious reputation. Paras were often used as a punishment squad, being sent into 'hardline' nationalist areas to subdue and intimidate opposition. While serving with the First Battalion of the Parachute Regiment in Belfast, Costos Georgiou acquired a 'hardman' reputation. He and other soldiers, seeking aggravation and violence with the local population, would often use unconventional methods to bring about a confrontation, 'Like pelting hotheaded mobs of Catholic youths with stones, provoking them into retaliation that could be matched with further violence'.[3]

Towards the end of his tour of duty, Georgiou and another soldier raided a post office using their army weapons. They were caught, dismissed from the army, and received five year jail sentences. 'Colonel Callan' turned up in Angola as a mercenary a few years later.

In 1994, three other British soldiers, serving in Cyprus with the Royal Greenjackets abducted Danish tour guide Louise Jenson. The three, Alan Ford, Justin Fowler and Jeff Pernell stripped her, sexually assaulted her, savagely beat her to death with an army issue spade and partially buried her. Louise Jenson's head was so badly damaged she could be identified only by a tattoo on her shoulder and a ring on one of her fingers. Rifleman Ford was already facing a charge of assault, accused of smashing a beer glass into the face of a British tourist, who had required 32 stitches to his wounds. Ford had not been confined to barracks 'because the case had not yet come to court'. According to evidence given during the soldiers' trial:

> Several barmen told the court that, less than two hours before the three
> allegedly killed the tour guide, they were on a drunken pub crawl in the two-
> star tourist resort of Ayia Napa and had danced in the streets.
>
> They detailed the astonishing quantities of alcohol that were consumed
> by the three. At one pub alone, Fowler and Pernell drank six or seven pints of
> beer each and Ford knocked back five or six whiskies, before each had three
> complimentary tequilas.[4]

The Greenjackets had fought in the Falklands and had just completed a tour of duty in Northern Ireland. *Observer* journalist Mike Theodoulou set out to get the soldiers' point of view and visited a bar frequented by British troops:

> And so it is that at Cozzi's pub, a drunken rifleman – who has just
> demanded another double vodka and lemonade – thrusts his sunburned nose
> inches from my face and barks: 'You fucker, you're making me really
> nervous, I mean I'm feeling really fucking aggressive. If you're a journalist,
> ask me a fucking question.'
>
> Did the Green Jackets like Cyprus?
>
> The answer was a quick and simple negative, without even the usual
> expletive. Most of the rank and file hate the island.
>
> … Hours after the drunken Green Jacket speaks to me, the whole
> regiment is called in by their commanding officer and warned not to speak to
> the press – as another soldier tells me at a different pub the following day.
>
> Many officers, who enjoy more gentlemanly pursuits such as polo,
> rambling and helping local charities, also cannot wait to leave. 'This incident
> was incredibly embarrassing after our superb record in Northern Ireland,'
> said one officer bitterly. 'Who remembers the medals we got there for
> gallantry now?'[5]

The actor, Tony Booth, became famous as the 'randy Scouse git' in the *Till Death*

Us Do Part TV series. In 1980, Booth, the father-in-law of Britain's Prime Minister Tony Blair, told how he was badly burned outside the door to his London flat.

During a drinking spree in Soho, Booth was introduced to two SAS soldiers who were just back from covert work in Ireland and who hinted about their involvement in undercover killings. Being 'interested in their work because I was writing a book and thought they could be useful', Booth invited the SAS men home to his flat. But, as he explained afterwards, things started to go wrong: 'we started squabbling and falling out and they kept calling me "Paddy" because of my Liverpool-Irish background. They were really nasty towards me, but I took them home just the same. That was nearly my fatal mistake.'[6] When they arrived at his Hampstead flat, Booth found he could not get in and decided that his partner, Susie, must have fallen asleep:

Our knocking and banging didn't wake her up. The two SAS mad-men said they'd smoke her out.

I told them not to be stupid and that I'd be able to get in through the loft.

I climbed up on top of some paraffin drums and started wriggling into the loft.

But when I was up there these two crackpots went into their commando routine.

They packed the door with rags, soaked them with heating paraffin that was stored on the landing – then set fire to them.

It all went horribly wrong.

One of the drums full of the stuff burst into flames. I was climbing on top of the drums to try to get into the loft. I fell right into the middle of one that was ablaze.

My boots filled up with the stuff and my feet were skinned down to the bone.

I was a burning torch from head to foot and those two crackpots just danced around, refusing to help, singing "Burn, you Paddy bastard, burn."

Somehow I got the flames out and came to in the intensive-care unit of a hospital with nearly half my body badly burned. It was the start of a lot of

Ex-soldiers go to war with the law on Civvy Street

E X-SOLDIERS are increasingly becoming involved in professional crime, according to police and probation officers and welfare workers. Some are using skills acquired in the army to carry out armed robberies with military precision.

With more than 32,000 servicemen leaving the armed forces in the past year, many without the prospect of regular work, the involvement of a growing minority in crime is now being recognised.

A probation officer with four former soldiers serving sentences for armed robbery as clients, says many ex-servicemen are unprepared for civilian life.

Speaking of an ex-soldier serving a three year sentence for robbery, she said: "...had prepared him for [...] that there were no jobs [...] He was used to a regular salary and had a wife and child to support. They come out with terrific expectations and then find out that life isn't like that."

Three other former soldiers who had served in Northern Ireland are now serving [...] year sentences for the armed robbery of a post office [...] had suffered trauma [...] their experiences [...] Ireland, she said [...] received no counselling [...]

From service to serving time

A number of recent court cases have involved ex-servicemen:

□ Sandhurst-trained Robert Cadiz (right) was given nine years for the armed robbery of the Clydesdale Bank in Aberdeen last month. He came from a privileged background but a need for excitement led him to crime.

Since [...] royal [...] jail [...]

threatening staff at Butlins Wonderwest World in Ayr with an imitation pistol.

□ In September, Donald McMillan, aged 33, a former tank driver, was found guilty of the murder of Helen Torbet and sentenced to life imprisonment.

□ In April, ex-army man Kurt Sandberg received a five-year jail term for forging [...] 5 million [...] an office [...]

Queen's man is fined

O NE of the Queen's bodyguards at Balmoral appeared in court yesterday.

Royal Scots private Derek MacGregor, 19, admitted striking a man outside a pub.

An officer told Inverness Sheriff Court the soldier had just been in Ulster.

"This is not an excuse but a possible explanation," he said.

MacGregor was [...]

YOU MADE ME A MONSTER!

Kissogram killer to sue for stress

A SCOTS soldier is suing the Government for turning him into a Civvy Street killer.

Hard-man Ray Jeffrey was dubbed the "kissogram killer".

He now says that the horrors of war changed his personality.

Jeffrey claims that atrocities during the Falklands conflict left him with post traumatic stress disorder, which was to blame for him carrying out a brutal slaying.

"I was turned from a professional killer into a monster," he says.

T RAGIC ex-squaddie Euart Kyles will take the mystery of his gun rampage through a Scots town to his grave.

Kyles, 18, blasted himself in the head after firing indiscriminately through shop windows in Ballater, Deeside.

He was rushed to hospital and put on life support machine but died on agony.[7]

In February 1990, fourteen-year-old Jamie McSloy was train-spotting on a school outing from Walkley, Yorkshire, to a rail museum in Reading. The railway platform was crowded and Jamie picked up what he thought was his sports bag. In fact, he had picked up a bag belonging to Northern Ireland veteran Scott Purnell, a twenty-year-old paratrooper. As the Sun reported, Purnell '**gripped** the terrified schoolboy in a headlock and **punched** him in the face at least eight times. When helpless Jamie collapsed, the para **jumped** on him with both feet and **stamped** on his head. Jamie – who had a similar bag to Purnell – has a fractured skull and internal bleeding' [emphasis in original].[8] Purnell escaped jail after the trial judge was shown a secret report from the army:

> Instead, Private Scott Purnell, who works in Army intelligence and has a medal for service in Ulster, was given two years' probation and ordered to pay his victim £2,000, after admitting grievous bodily harm.
>
> ...Assistant Recorder Peter Cooper told Purnell, of 1st Battalion of the Parachute Regiment, Aldershot: 'I accept that you lost your reason and sense of control. The matters which caused this have not been touched on in open court but I accept them.'[9]

From Angola to Cyprus to back home in Britain some Northern Ireland veterans have left a trail of death and destruction. Louise Jenson, Tony Booth and Jamie McSloy were just some of the many civilians who have suffered in violent incidents involving these returning soldiers. Often, this aggro is dished out by squaddies brutalized by their training and tours of duty, who are liable to express their frustrations and release their pent-up emotions by inflicting violence on anyone they meet. In other cases, the veterans are suffering from psychological problems resulting from their service in conflict situations.

In April 1989, violence stemming from the war in Northern Ireland disturbed the peace in an idyllic part of the English countryside. Gunfire rang out in a tranquil Suffolk village, sending the local people scurrying for cover and requesting help. This incident did not involve the IRA: the violence came from a returning British soldier:

When Corporal Michael King bought himself out of the British Army in 1988 he left the barracks in County Armagh with only one intention: to escape from what seemed to him an intolerable life. His two years of infantry service in Northern Ireland – street patrols, mortar attacks, deaths of fellow soldiers – had stretched his nerves to breaking point. He had resolved to abandon an eight-year military career, his friends in the regiment and to start anew on the mainland.[10]

He had settled happily into civilian life, living with his wife in the village of Nayland. All was going well until, strolling home one Sunday afternoon, King suddenly believed he was back in the war zone on active service. Imagining IRA men in the surrounding area he ran home and took out his shotgun and what he had left of his army equipment. While his terrified wife hid in a cupboard, he set up a firing position at the front window of the flat and started shooting. His first shots hit the vicarage, attracting the attention of other villagers who summoned help. Soon King was surrounded by police squads, including marksmen prepared to shoot.

Michael King had suffered a flashback – one of the symptoms of Post-traumatic Stress Disorder (PTSD). Without any knowledge of this condition, he desperately tried to come to terms with what was happening and end his siege:

... worst of all he could find no explanation for his loss of control.

Knowing nothing of PTSD or its treatment, he concluded himself to be 'beyond help', a danger to society, and called on the police marksmen to shoot him – 'take me out'. But the police had sensed that the threat to the public had ceased, and that the only life in grave danger was King's – at his own hand. Throughout the night two police officers talked to him and finally convinced him of the option of surrender.[11]

In April 1990, Michael King appeared before Ipswich Crown Court and pleaded guilty to charges of criminal damage. He entered a plea of mitigation that he had been suffering from PTSD, the first time this argument had been used in a British court. Sentencing King to three-years probation, contingent upon him continuing a course of therapy, Justice John Turner said, 'I am now satisfied you were suffering from a serious condition of trauma associated with your service with Her Majesty's Army ... and there is no real risk of a repeat providing you undertake therapy.'[12]

The Universal Soldier

In recent years, graphic press and TV coverage has created indelible images of a series of tragic disasters: the sinking of the *Herald of Free Enterprise* at Zeebrugge and of the *Marchioness* on the Thames; rail disasters like those at King's Cross and Clapham; football tragedies at Bradford and Hillsborough; and the explosion of Pan Am flight 103 from the skies onto Lockerbie. With the public feeling sympathy, sorrow and sometimes anger, there was also a growing realisation that survivors – and often rescuers and witnesses – could afterwards suffer severe psychological problems. It also became apparent that expert diagnosis and treatment were required to aid recovery. Gradually, official recognition has meant that short and long-term counselling is now often provided and, in some cases, compensation has been paid for mental suffering.

Thankfully, most of us go through life without having to face such situations. Soldiers, however, thrust into conflicts that continually throw up violent and bloody actions, cannot only expect to experience traumatic events – their whole *raison d'être* is to train for and take part in them. Michael King was just one of many soldiers who have suffered from PTSD and other rehabilitation problems after tours of duty in Northern Ireland. Because of the macho culture that prevails in the army, most soldiers think it would be a sign of weakness to admit to showing symptoms. They need help from the Ministry of Defence (MoD) and their army units. But, as King's experiences prove, they are not getting it:

> In 1984, just after the Harrods bombing, King had experienced an
> earlier, lesser episode of PTSD. It happened while he was on leave from his
> battalion's intelligence section. He was arrested in an abandoned house
> which he deludedly believed to be the base of the bombers. 'It came from all
> the same symptoms, lack of sleep, isolation, and a sense of guilt at why the
> English police, in the capital city of my country, should have to deal with a
> problem I should be dealing with as a member of the military. The civilian
> psychiatrist put it down to depression but told me to consult my battalion's

medical officer on return to base. When I told him the symptoms, he said,
"Yeah, no problem, we're being posted to Ireland, let's just leave it there.'"

So, instead of a medical discharge, King received a two-year tour in
Northern Ireland. Of the mental agony leading up to his second episode,
King says: 'If there had been a place, a person or even a telephone line I
could have called when my life was ruled by PTSD symptoms, then all this
would probably never have happened.'[13]

For us to understand the relevance today of PTSD for some of the soldiers who
have served in Northern Ireland, we need to uncover the hidden history of the
psychological problems that wars have caused in those who have fought in them.
From very early times, physical conflict between peoples has induced shock
among combatants. In the Roman legions the bearers of the eagle standards were
chosen from the best of the veteran centurions. But sometimes even they broke in
battle. During the decade-long wars in Gaul, the historian Suetonius recorded
that twice the Caesar tried to stop eagle-bearers from fleeing from the battlefield,
on one occasion being lucky to escape being struck by the sharp end of a standard.
In the other incident, the Caesar was left holding the standard after it was thrust
into his hands by the fleeing bearer he had tried to stop.

For some soldiers their problems did not end with the battle. Afterwards,
they often experienced difficulty coming to terms with their actions and the horrors they had witnessed. Back home, family and friends became alarmed by the
changes in the veteran's character. In Shakespeare's *Henry IV, Part One*, Lady
Percy expresses concern about her warrior husband Hotspur:

> O, my good lord, why are you thus alone?
> For what offence have I this fortnight been
> A banish'd woman from my Harry's bed?
> Tell me, sweet lord, what is't that takes from thee
> Thy stomach, pleasure and thy golden sleep?
> Why dost thou bend thine eyes upon the earth,
> And start so often when thou sittest alone?
> Why hast thou lost the fresh blood in thy cheeks;

And given my treasures and my rights of thee
To thick-eyed musing and cursed melancholy?
In thy faint slumbers I by thee have watch'd,
And heard thee murmur tales of iron wars,
Speak terms of manage to thy bounding steed,
Cry 'Courage! to the field!' And thou hast talk'd
Of sallies and retires, of trenches, tents,
Of palisadoes, frontiers, parapets,
Of basilisks, of cannon, culverin,
Of prisoners' ransom, and of soldiers slain,
And all the currents of a heady fight.
Thy spirit within thee hath been so at war,
And thus hath so bestirr'd thee in thy sleep,
That beads of sweat have stood upon thy brow
Like bubbles in a late-disturbed stream,
And in thy face strange motions have appear'd,
Such as we see when men restrain their breath
On some great sudden hest.
O, what portents are these?
Some heavy business hath my lord in hand,
And I must know it, else he loves me not.[14]

Lady Percy's description of Hotspur's condition clearly showed him to be suffering from post-battle problems: he preferred to be alone, and had lost his appetite for food and sex; he appeared depressed and was easily startled; he was experiencing problems sleeping; when sleep came it was troubled, with murmurings and nightmares about the wars. Of course, the condition was not recognised at that time. But, Shakespeare has provided us with one of the first descriptions of the type of psychological disorders that occurred among men who had fought in brutal wars.

Military leaders usually regarded the appearance of mental problems in ordinary soldiers as cowardice, or as resulting from lapses in discipline. The American Civil War pitched large armies using modern weapons against each other. But attitudes about soldiers who suffered psychological problems remained unchanged:

> If a soldier's behaviour was sufficiently bizarre and dramatic, he could
> simply be classified as one of the 2,603 cases of insanity recorded in the
> Federal army during the war. But if the soldier was chronically morose, lost
> his appetite and physical stamina, and was unable to function as well as his
> comrades, he became a candidate for the more opaque diagnosis of
> 'nostalgia'. Described by surgeons as a particularly debilitating form of
> homesickness, nostalgia was regarded chiefly as a 'camp disease', marked by
> lassitude of the spirit, complicated by the boredom of long bivouacs and the
> rigours of marching. But neither nostalgia nor any other mental ailment was
> ever attributed to the rigours of combat itself. On the contrary, T J Calhoun,
> an assistant surgeon with the Army of the Potomac, advised his colleagues
> that if the soldier could not be 'laughed out of it by his comrades' or by
> 'appeals to his manhood', then a good dose of battle was the best 'curative'.[15]

Throughout the centuries Britain's forces were often engaged in conflicts overseas. After wars, the streets back home were often filled with discharged veterans who the authorities did little to help. Many were crippled, others were feared, being quick to fly into rages and liable to use violence. Some were mentally disturbed by their experiences. Ordinary soldiers received no great reward for their service or disabilities, so many resorted to begging. Henry Mayhew described some Crimea veterans:

> The first, or soldier proper, has all the evidence of drill and barrack life
> about him; the eye that always 'fronts' the person he addresses; the spare
> habit, high cheekbones, regulation whisker, stiff chin ... He carries his papers
> with him, and when he has been wounded or seen service, is modest and
> retiring as to his share of glory. ... Try him which way you will he will never
> confess that he has killed a man. He compensates himself for his silence on
> the subject of fighting by his excessive grumbling as to his provisions,
> quarters, etc., to which he has been forced to submit in the course of his
> career. ... Ragged though he be, there is a certain smartness about the soldier
> proper, observable in the polish of his boots, the cock of his cap, and the

HENRY IV, PART I
by William Shakespeare
Act II, Scene III

Lady Percy (to her husband, Hotspur):

O, my good lord, why are you thus alone?   *isolates*
For what offence have I this fortnight been
A banish'd woman from my Harry's bed?   *↓ sex*
Tell me, sweet lord, what is't that takes from thee   *↓ appetite*
Thy stomach[1], pleasure and thy golden sleep?   *↓ sleep*
Why dost thou bend thine eyes upon the earth,   *depressed*
And start so often when thou sit'st alone?   *easily startled*
Why hast thou lost the fresh blood in thy cheeks;
And given my treasures and my rights of thee
To thick-eyed musing and cursed melancholy?   *preoccupied*
In thy faint slumbers I by thee have watch'd,
And heard thee murmur tales of iron wars;   *nightmares*
Speak terms of manage[2] to thy bounding steed;
Cry 'Courage! to the field!' And thou hast talk'd   *Talks in*
Of sallies and retires, of trenches, tents,   *sleep D*
Of palisadoes[3], frontiers, parapets[4],   *war.*
Of basilisks[5], of cannon, culverin[5],
Of prisoners' ransom and of soldiers slain,
And all the currents of a heady fight.
Thy spirit within thee hath been so at war
And thus hath so bestirr'd thee in thy sleep,
That beads of sweat have stood upon thy brow,   *night sweats*
Like bubbles in a late-disturbed stream;
And thy face strange motions have appear'd,
Such as we see when men restrain their breath   *anxious,*
On some great sudden hest.   *tense*
O, what portents are these?
Some heavy business hath my lord in hand,
And I must know it, else he loves me not.

[1] stomach, Appetite
[2] manage, Horsemanship
[3] palisadoes, Stakes in the ground to stop a charge
[4] parapets, A defensive wall or elevation
[5] basilisks...culverin, Small and large cannon

Butchers of Cyprus face life in cushy prison

VICTIM ... tour guide Louise

Para butchers wife and her pal then jumps to his death

GRIM ... of the two murdered women

...bing himself...

...park

ARLISON

...best pal Alexia

"hello', she was very nice."
...Another neighbour said she
...ntroned Darren, known as
...ish family..."

HOR
HOU
GIRL
FEAR

...my
...off
...dier
...o hit
...en

R hero
...e for attacking
...man won't be
...unished by...

A FATHER killed his wife, teenage
daughter and himself
shotgun horror early yesterday.

And the massacre came only hours af...
girl said she had been scared by...
fortune teller told her about her f...
future.

The triple tragedy was discovered whe...
Downes, 14, ran
screaming from the
family home in the
fishing village of
Portavogie, Co Down.

Police then found the
bodies of Stuart Downes,
41, his wife Elizabeth,
37, and 17-year-old
daughter Joanne.

LATE

Joanne's friend, Naomi
Palmer, said later: "She
told me she had been to a
fortune teller and was
really scared.

"She said she had been
told mostly about her
family. She never got
on with them and there
were always arguments.

"She had been staying
out quite late at the
weekends and did not
seem to want to go
home."

Neighbours said
Englishman Downes was
a former soldier who
had served in Ulster
before moving from East
Belfast and setting up a
car restoring business.

Downes had been
drinking before the
shootings, according to
the neighbours.

'Reaper' maniac gets life

A SOLDIER wept as he
admitted murdering his
wife and was jailed for
life yesterday.

Patrick Gavin – who
butchered wife Sharon
with a Bowie knife he
called the Grim Reaper
– broke down on the
second day of his trial at
Nottingham Crown
Court.

Gavin, 22, went
berserk after Sharon –
also 22 – set up home
with another man. A
charge of raping his
wife will lie on the file.

Squaddie blew wife apart in bed romp'

Grenade blast during row

A BRITISH soldier told a court
yesterday how his wife was
blown to pieces as they
struggled violently in bed over
a hand grenade.

Anke Eddowes, 27, died instantly
when it exploded after slipping into
her cleavage.

The prosecution alleges Lance Corporal Phillip Eddowes – who lost a
hand and an eye in the blast – pulled
out the pin and placed the grenade in
her dress after a heated argument
about splitting up.

But Eddowes, 29 who denied

manslaughter, claimed it accidently
went off while he was trying to
frighten his wife.

The soldier, serving with the 33rd
Engineer Regiment in Hanover,
Germany – Anke's home country –
said she walked out in October
after he hit her when he suspected
she was having an affair.

Exploded

She returned two days later to col-
lect some belongings and he went
into the bedroom with her, locked
the door and pleaded with her to
stay. He took the grenade – which
he had found while clean-
ing inside a British Army
tank – from a drawer and
threatened to pull out
the pin if she left.

Anke tried to grab...

disposition of the leather strap under his lower lip. He invariably carries a stick, and when a soldier passes him, casts on him an odd sort of look, half envying, half pitying, as if he said, 'Though you are better fed than I, you are not so free!'

... The second sort of soldier-beggar is one of the most dangerous and violent mendicants. Untamable even by regimental discipline, insubordinate by nature, he has been thrust out from the army to prey on society. He begs but seldom, and is dangerous to meet with after dark on a lonely road, or in a sequestered lane.[16]

Many of the men in the latter category had probably been brutalized by the savage fighting they had taken part in. Some will have been suffering from psychological problems due to their war experiences.

Shell Shock

During the First World War, the casualties suffered on even a single day were frequently enormous, and a system had to be put in place to deal with the injured. There was a great expansion of medical facilities. In the British army area in France the number of medical officers increased from 200 to over 10,000. Clearing stations were set up just behind the front lines with base hospitals to the rear, and wounded soldiers could be moved back to the more extensive medical facilities in Britain if that proved necessary.

While humanitarian concern for the wounded motivated many of the doctors and nurses, there was another reason for the vast expansion of the medical network. During the great battles, high numbers of casualties reduced fighting units to a skeleton, depleting armies and rendering them impotent. The military command required an efficient system for clearing the badly wounded from the front and for quickly treating those with lesser injuries to ensure their speedy return to the trenches. Soldiers soon learnt to recognise the type of wounds that would ensure their evacuation from the horror of the front for good. To have a 'Blighty one' was regarded by many men as preferable to staying on in the trenches.

By the end of the war, some 80,000 front-line troops had been treated for various types of psychological breakdowns, which became known collectively as 'shell shock'. At first, it was thought that the cause of shell shock lay in gases escaping from exploding shells. Others thought that shock waves from the explosions were responsible. Various theories were put forward to explain shell shock:

> For conventional medico-psychiatry, the First World War disturbances presented real diagnostic difficulties: how to make sense of this 'no man's land' of illness, which seemed to negate commonly held beliefs about valour and masculinity, and to defy the prevailing organic models of insanity and its aetiology? The idea that the shellshocked were all hereditary degenerates or that their condition could be put down to the commotional effects of exploding shells on the central nervous system proved increasingly unsustainable. Yet shellshock could not be explained away as malingering. It blurred the distinctions between neurosis and insanity – and it was a crisis on a massive scale. According to one account in 1916, shellshock cases constituted up to 40 per cent of the casualties from heavy fighting zones; more alarmingly still, officers seemed especially prone to it. Army statistics revealed that officers were more than twice as likely to suffer from mental breakdown on the battlefield as men of the ranks.[17]

In the British Army, senior officers tended to regard any sign of weakness among their troops as cowardice. So, ordinary soldiers were on the receiving end of harsh discipline and military courts when they were unable to function as soldiers due to mental stress. Given the numbers of physically injured, perhaps it is not surprising that little sympathy would be spared for those suffering from invisible wounds. This harsh view was alleviated, to some extent, by the realisation that officers appeared to be more susceptible to shell shock than ordinary soldiers. By the end of the first year of the war reports from the Army Medical Corps revealed that 7 to 10 per cent of all officer patients and 3 to 4 per cent of non-commissioned soldiers undergoing treatment were suffering from mental problems.

Lower ranking officers had to share the hell of the front line, while the General Staff wallowed in the comparative luxury of safe base areas. As the British Army adhered rigidly to the class system, some junior officers started to take issue with aspects of the war and a few developed kindred feelings for the soldiers they commanded. Siegfried Sassoon, one of these ex-public-school officers who expressed their disillusion in poetry, was known as 'mad Jack' to his men in the Royal Welsh Fusiliers. He was a model front-line officer, who led with such bravado that he was awarded a Military Cross. In 1917, recovering from war wounds in a British hospital, Sassoon wrote 'A Soldier's Declaration', described by him as 'an act of wilful defiance of military authority', claiming that 'the War is being deliberately prolonged by those who have the power to end it':

> I am a soldier, convinced that I am acting on behalf of soldiers. I believe
> that this War, upon which I entered as a war of defence and liberation, has
> now become a war of aggression and conquest. I believe that the purposes for
> which I and my fellow-soldiers entered upon this War should have been so
> clearly stated as to have made it impossible for them to be changed without
> our knowledge, and that, had this been done, the objects which actuated us
> would now be attainable by negotiation.
>
> I have seen and endured the suffering of the troops, and I can no longer
> be a party to prolonging those sufferings for ends which I believe to be evil
> and unjust.
>
> I am not protesting against the military conduct of the War, but against
> the political errors and insincerities for which the fighting men are being
> sacrificed.
>
> On behalf of those who are suffering now, I make this protest against the
> deception which is being practised on them. Also I believe that it may help to
> destroy the callous complacence with which the majority of those at home
> regard the continuance of agonies which they do not share, and which they
> have not sufficient imagination to realise.

Sassoon's declaration was published as a letter in *The Times*. He fully expected to be court-martialled, and hoped to use the process to focus attention on securing a quick end to the war. Instead, a friend and fellow officer, Robert Graves, arranged for him to appear before a medical board. The authorities were happy to go along with this, and the board immediately sent him to Craiglockhart war hospital in Edinburgh as a shell-shock case. This successfully curtailed Sassoon's protest, suggesting that his anti-war views came from someone suffering mental problems.

In Craiglockhart, which he nicknamed 'Dottyville', Sassoon saw at first hand how the the war had ravaged the minds of some of his fellow front line officers. Sassoon wrote of the hospital; 'The doctors did everything possible to counteract gloom, and the wrecked faces were outnumbered by those who were emerging from their nervous disorders. ... But by night they lost control and the hospital became sepulchral and oppressive with saturations of war experience. ... One became conscious that the place was full of men whose slumbers were morbid and terrifying – men muttering uneasily or suddenly crying out in their sleep.' Sassoon expressed anger against those who had caused the suffering of his fellow officers:

> Shell shock. How many a brief bombardment had its long-delayed after-effect in the minds of these survivors, many of whom had looked at their companions and laughed while the inferno did its best to destroy them. Not then was their evil hour; but now; now, in the sweating suffocation of nightmare, in paralysis of limbs, in the stammering of dislocated speech. Worst of all, in the disintegration of those qualities through which they had been so gallant and selfless and uncomplaining – this, in the finer types of men, was the unspeakable tragedy of shell-shock; it was in this that their humanity had been outraged by those explosives which were sanctioned and glorified by the Churches; it was thus that their self-sacrifice was mocked and maltreated – they, who in the name of righteousness had been sent out to maim and slaughter their fellow-men. In the name of civilisation these soldiers had been martyred, and it remained for civilisation to prove that their martyrdom wasn't a dirty swindle.[18]

Sassoon was especially incensed by the jingoistic support the war received back home. He attacked this attitude, especially as expressed in the music-halls, in his poem 'Blighters':

> The House is crammed: tier upon tier they grin
> And crackle at the Show, while prancing ranks
> Of harlots shrill the chorus, drunk with din;
> 'We're sure the Kaiser loves our dear old Tanks!'

I'd like to see a Tank come down the stalls,
Lurching to rag-time tunes, or 'Home, sweet Home',
And there'd be no more jokes in Music-halls
To mock the riddled corpses round Bapaume.

The 'Sticker'

A fellow patient at Craiglockhart was Wilfred Owen from the Manchester Regiment, whom Sassoon encouraged to write poems about the war. Owen was suffering from shell shock and encapsulated his experiences in these verses from his poem 'Mental Cases':

- These are men whose minds the Dead have
ravished.
Memory fingers in their hair of murders,
Multitudinous murders they once witnessed.
Wading sloughs of flesh these helpless wander,
Treading blood from lungs that had loved laughter.
Always they must see these things and hear them,
Batter of guns and shatter of flying muscles,
Carnage incomparable, and human squander
Rucked too thick for these men's extrication.

Therefore still their eyeballs shrink tormented
Back into their brains, because on their sense
Sunlight seems a blood-smear; night comes blood-
black;
Dawn breaks open like a wound that bleeds afresh.
- Thus their heads wear this hilarious, hideous,
Awful falseness of the set-smiling corpses.
- Thus their hands are plucking at each other;
Picking at the rope-knouts of their scourging;
Snatching after us who smote them, brother,

Pawing at us who dealt them war and madness.

Owen is suggesting that many of his fellow soldiers were affected psycho-logically by 'murders' – the death and destruction that they dished out to their enemy as well as by that which was inflicted on them. Certainly, any soldier who served in the trenches for any length of time must have witnessed appalling hor-ror. Through the realisation of what conditions at the front were really like and the evident effects they had on the returning men, the British public gradually came to accept shell shock as a condition which could affect any soldier. In Europe, peo-ple like Sigmund Freud, the father of psychoanalysis, took up the issue:

> The war, as Freud noted in the introduction to a psychoanalytic study of shellshock, 'was not without an important influence on the spread of psychoanalysis', because medical men 'who had hitherto held back from any approach to psychoanalytic theory were brought into close contact with them when in the course of their duty as army doctors they were obliged to deal with war neuroses'. The book had arisen from contributions to the fifth International Psychoanalytical Congress held in Budapest in late September 1918. A symposium had been held on 'The Psychoanalysis of War Neuroses'.

> ... official observers from the highest quarters of the Central European Powers were present as observers at the Budapest Congress. In Freud's words, 'The hopeful result of this contact was that the establishment of psychoanalytic Centres was promised, at which analytically trained physicians would have leisure and opportunity for studying the nature of these puzzling disorders [the war neuroses] and the therapeutic effect exercised on them by psychoanalysis.'

> Before these proposals could be put into effect, however, 'the war came to an end, the state organisations collapsed and interest in the war neuroses gave place to other concerns'.[19]

Throughout the war, the British top brass were worried by the numbers of troops who appeared to be affected – to a greater or lesser degree – by shell shock. As in other wars, many generals thought the answer was to call those suffering

General Routine Order No. 2384

CLASSIFICATION AND DISPOSAL OF OFFICERS AND OTHER RANKS WHO WITHOUT ANY VISIBLE WOUND BECOME NON-EFFECTIVE FROM PHYSICAL CONDITIONS CLAIMED OR PRESUMED TO HAVE ORIGINATED FROM THE EFFECTS OF BRITISH OR ENEMY WEAPONS IN ACTION.

(1) All officers and other ranks who become non-effective in the above category, and whose transfer from their unit or division is unavoidable, will be sent to the Special Hospital set apart for their reception under the order of the Army Commander.

(2) The Regimental Medical Officer, or officer commanding a medical unit, who in the first instance deals with a case which it is necessary to transfer to the Special Hospital, will not record any diagnosis. He will enter on the Field Medical Card or other transfer paper the letters 'NYDN' (Not Yet Diagnosed, Nervous) only, and note any definitely known facts as to the true origin or the previous history of the case. . .

(5) . . . In no circumstances whatever will the expression 'shell-shock' be used verbally or be recorded in any regimental or other casualty report, or in any hospital or other medical document, except in cases classified by the order of the officer commanding the Special Hospital. The DAG, GHQ, 3rd Echelon, will notify the commanding officer of the unit of any case so classified.

(6) These orders do not apply to cases of gas poisoning, which will be dealt with as heretofore.

(7) All previous orders and instructions on this subject are cancelled.

A British Army Order of June 7 1917

ANGUISH A SOLDIER SUFFERED

SOLDIER John Henderson had to leave the Black Watch after his best friend was killed by Irish terrorists.

Then the break-up of his marriage added to his mental stress.

And it all spilled out while he was staying with his sister in Pauldhouse, a court heard this week.

He took his brother-in-law's car and crashed it into a ditch on a lonely country road.

But when two passers-by helped him get it back on the road, he produced a replica 9mm Magnum pistol and started firing blank cartridges.

Twenty-three-year-old Henderson, now living in Perthshire, appeared from custody at Linlithgow Sheriff Court on Monday and admitted a series of motoring charges as well as brandishing the gun and escaping from police.

Fiscal depute Carol Rowe said that, at first, the two youths did not report the incident with the pistol.

But when they drove along the same road later and saw the car in a ditch again — on the opposite side of the road and

pointing the other way — they told the police what had happened.

In the meantime, officers had gone to see Henderson because of his report that the car was stolen.

And he had produced the gun for them, she said, "making comments about how they would give the thief a fright."

He was given "a severe reprimand" and the officers left the house. But after speaking to the two youths they returned and arrested Henderson for taking the car.

He was put in a cell at Fauldhouse police station and was making a lot of noise, the fiscal said, shouting and banging on the door.

When he suddenly went quiet, officers went to investigate and found the vibration had sprung the lock of the cell door. The station's back door was unlocked from the inside and Henderson was gone. He was arrested at his sister's house later.

Sheriff Marcus Stone called for reports on Henderson and released him on bail until November 19.

2 Brit soldiers held in Falls sex assault

NIAGARA FALLS, Ont. (CP) — Two British soldiers have been charged with sexual assault after a woman said she was attacked on a Niagara Falls street.

Police say the woman, 18, was walking on a downtown street at 1:30 a.m. Saturday when a man touched her in "a sexual manner." The attacker fled when a male friend of the woman chased him, police said.

While the friend was in pursuit, a second man allegedly assaulted her in the same manner.

Paul Corlett, 24, and Paul Simmons, 28, were turned over to military police from Canadian Forces Base Borden, where they are stationed.

The Sun 28/6/93

Derry horror turned soldier into fugitive

A YOUNG British soldier became a real life version of the television thriller "The Fugitive," a court was told yesterday.

It happened after the soldier Trooper John Oliver (27), of the Household Cavalry, drove through the horror of Bloody Sunday in Derry, when demonstrators were shot dead by the British army Para chute Regiment. Hysterical women claimed at him and begged him to "save my babies".

Trooper Oliver had been in the North just three days. Then he went on the run for five years.

At a magistrates' court in Middlesbrough yesterday, Mr Peter Boddy, defending, said that how Oliver's greatest fear was to be returned to the army. Bloody Sunday had been horrific to him. He could not face going back in the army.

But the magistrates fined him and ordered that he be returned to the army. Last week he waited in a police cell for an escort to take him

Soldier shot

A soldier was seriously ill in hospital last night after being shot by a colleague at the Army base at Castledillon, County Armagh.

Private David Carrington, aged 19, from Derbyshire, was found dead yesterday after a four-day siege at Dhekelia barracks in Cyprus which began when he briefly kidnapped four women soldiers. No cause of death was given.

FORMER soldier James Robertson tried to drown his horror memories of Northern Ireland in drink, a court heard yesterday.

But after downing EIGHTEEN cans of lager and a BOTTLE of vodka, he and another man robbed a shop using a fake firearm.

Soldier jailed for 10 years

A young soldier whose home-made bomb seriously injured a four-year-old boy was jailed for 10 years at the Old Bailey yesterday.

Royal Green Jacket James Cobb, 19, planted the device near his parents' home hoping it would make a "big bang". But Michael Walsh picked up the bomb in a plastic milk container outside his home in Putney, south London. It exploded, turning him into a human fireball, and he will be permanently disfigured.

Cobb only admitted making the bomb with materials stolen from Army stores, but he was also found guilty of using explosives with intent to maim, burn, disfigure or cause serious bodily harm.

Soldiers jailed

A Belfast Crown Court yesterday heard how three British soldiers had escaped from their barracks on January 19th last and had carried out hijackings and other offences. Private Clive Bruce (21), of the Green Howards, was sentenced to eight years, imprisonment, Private William Bairstow (20), also of the Green Howards, was sentenced to five years in jail and Sapper Adrian Jones (19) received six years in jail after the judge said that he was the only one of the trio who had any prospect of a suc[...] Army career.

"Firearms were involved," said [...] [Mini]stry of Defence

Gulf heroes held

Desert Rats face gun raids probe

THREE Desert Rat heroes from the Gulf War are being held on suspicion of armed robbery.

Their arrest follows a series of raids on cash from takeaways in the Hanover area of Germany, where thousands of British soldiers are stationed.

are privates from the 1st Battalion of the Staffordshire Regiment.

The[y] returned back from the [...] line throughout the Gulf conflict.

[...] are urging Defence [...] Tom King to [...] [pris]oners

'Lock me away!!!'

□ SOLDIER Stephen Phillips was sent to prison for six months by an East London judge for stealing cars.

Phillips asked for a prison sentence because he couldn't face another year of duty with the army in Northern Ireland.

He went absent without leave and stole cars so that he would be discharged.

Soldier face[s] robbery charg[e]

Belfast: A Scottish soldier serving here was accused yesterday of using his army rifle to commit armed robberies and to resist arrest.

William Ennis (20) from Glasgow, a private in the Royal Highland Fusiliers, was charged with armed raids at an insurance company's offices on the University Road and a Chinese restaurant on Woodstock Road in whose £700 was stolen.

When the offences place last year, Ennis stationed at Palace Holywood, and his now in Berlin.

Ennis, who [...] clothes, said from [...] would not have used [...] resist arrest[...] [d]eny of "big bang"[...]

He was [...] [B]elfast

Rape b[y] soldier is jailed

A DRUNKEN soldier who dragged a girl off the street and tried to rape her was jailed four years yesterday. She was saved from death by two labourers, a court heard.

Paul Saunders, 23, of Spennymoor Road, Catterick, [...] Ann [...] was held on leave from the King's Own Scottish Borderers. The High Court at Kilmarnock heard he [...] spent £80 on an all-day drinking bout

Soldier on murder charge

A SOLDIER was charged with murder after a shooting incident in Northern Ireland yesterday morning in which another soldier was killed.

Sapper Robert Paul Adams, of the Royal Engineers, was remanded in custody during an appearance in a special court

Call for Army death probe

AN MP has demanded an MoD probe into a Scots squaddie's death. Black Watch soldier Sean Murphy, 20, was shot in the head with his own rifle while on guard duty at Glencorse Barracks, Penicuik, Midlothian.

Central Fife MP Henry McLeish yesterday asked

circumstances of Glenrothes lance [...] ral's death.

McLeish said: serious concern safety measures surrounding the incident live ammunition.

An army spokesman used to discuss the circumstances [...] police probe [...]

Soldier who was racially abused wins fight for compensation

A FORMER army private who suffered racial abuse won £500 compensation yesterday in the first case of its kind to be heard by the Army Board.

It ruled in Stephen Anderson's favour on eight of his 13 complaints, the Ministry of Defence said. The Board had refused Mr Anderson redress in 1989, but was forced to reconsider under procedures laid down by the High Court which has

that army procedures fell below the standards of fairness and justice accorded civilians.

Mr Anderson, aged 25, who joined the Devon and Dorset regiment in 1983, was the only black soldier in his platoon.

He said he suffered racial abuse in 1985 at Brook Barracks in West Germany when a lance-corporal and two other soldiers dragged him from his bed, after a drinking spree, punched and kicked him, and

[P]ARA [B]EATING BO[Y]

A PARATROOPER who stamped on a 14-year-old boy's head escaped jail yesterday after the judge was shown a secret report from the Army.

Jamie Molloy was left with a fractured skull and internal bleeding from the horrific attack. Clive Bruce tried to pin the soldier's beating for his mistake.

Wilkinson said 20-year-old Army

The assault took place at Reading railway station in February.

Purnell, based with the 1st Battalion of the Parachute Regiment in Aldershot, told police: "I went over the top. That's the way I have been brought up!"

The para, said to have carried out intelligence work in Ulster

Ulster hero fined £750 for glass attack in pub

A SOLDIER who saved the lives of seven men in Ulster was fined £750 for a pub attack yesterday.

Ian Harvey, 29, a corporal with the 1st Battalion, the King's Own Scottish Borderers, was also ordered to pay £750 compensation to his victim, Richard Murphy.

Mr Murphy needed 15 stitches in three face cuts after he was hit with a beer glass in the Good Companions pub at Oxgangs, Edinburgh, in April, 1991, the city's sheriff court was told.

Duncan Hughes, defending, said that before a spell in Northern Ireland at the end of 1989, Harvey's wife, who looked after him, had formed a relationship with

After the incident, the court heard that Harvey received psychiatric treatment for trauma. "On his return from Northern Ireland, he said he simply could not get out of his mind the affair that was going on prior to his going and he was in a confused state of mind," said Mr Hughes.

Harvey's wife later left him, the court was told.

The attack took place about a month after his return from Northern Ireland, when Harvey saw Murphy in the pub.

Mr Hughes claimed that Harvey initially intended emptying a pint over Murphy but "flipped" and hit him in the face with the beer glass.

"There had been no contact

"His intention was to stay in the army, which he sees as being his life," said Mr Hughes.

Sheriff David Crowe told Harvey: "You are a professional soldier. You are trained to react in certain circumstances and the hallmark of a professional soldier is to know when to draw the line."

Harvey had "lost the head" on the night in the pub.

Despite the serious nature of the offence and Harvey's previous convictions, including one for assault, the sheriff said a custodial sentence was not appropriate. "I am not going to send the career of someone who is otherwise an excellent soldier," he added.

from the disorder 'cowards' and 'malingerers' and punish them severely. One commander had shellshock cases tied to the barbed wire protecting the trenches, in order to 'install backbone' and act as a warning to others. For similar reasons, over three hundred British soldiers were shot for 'cowardice' and 'desertion'. Most were suffering from shell shock.[20]

In Britain, at the end of the war, political battles were fought in Parliament and in the medical establishment to prevent the practice of the worst cases of shell-shocked soldiers being designated insane and committed to asylums. Many in the British army command still refused to accept shell shock as a diagnosis, and when they looked at the problem, class prejudice was evident:

... the War Office Committee of Inquiry into Shellshock under the chairmanship of Lord Southborough in 1922 entertained but then rejected Freud's therapy, or at least the 'sanitised' version they had been offered by Head and Rivers [British shellshock doctors]. The committee declared that Jews, the Irish and the working classes were more likely to break down, as were 'artistic types' and 'imaginative city-dwellers' and other such 'highly strung' people.[21]

Ironically, at the end of the Great War, some of Britain's front line veterans were recruited back into uniform as a back-up force to the Royal Irish Constabulary and sent to Ireland to fight Irish nationalists. Ex-soldiers joined the infamous Black and Tans, while ex-officers enlisted with the more elite Auxiliaries. Many of the men had been brutalized by years of trench warfare, some still suffered from shell shock, and both outfits quickly gained a reputation for using excessive violence. The Women's International League, formed by suffragettes opposed to the First World War, commented in their monthly news-sheet:

The British Government has sent to Ireland to reinforce the army of occupation a number of soldiers (known as 'Black and Tan') who have been through the war and re-enlisted. Their outrages upon the Irish people – burning of villages and creameries, terrorisation of inhabitants (bed-ridden old folk, women in childbed, children) under a prolonged torture of their victims – are such as suggest to many people that these men are the scum of the prisons and that the Government, which liberates certain criminals in order to use them as agents provocateurs, is liberating others on condition that they enlist in the army.

Whether this be so or not in some cases, it is not necessary to assume that it is so in general. There is a most enlightening letter on Shell-shock by Dr. C. M. Wilson in the *Times* of September 22nd, discussing what types of men can get through the strain of modern warfare and by what means they can be trained to do so. He writes:

"The 'sticker' was just one who managed to cut off all, or at least many, of the messages from the outer world that reached the brain at times like these and destroyed its balance. His business was to become insensitive, to give up thinking; for him the fewer aspects life presented, the longer he lasted. The wise man lived only for the hour. We have to determine whether the proposed methods of preparing the mind of the soldier do actually conduce to the state here depicted, or whether they breed that habit of introspection which was the sure and certain herald of individual defeat."

This analysis is acute and absolutely correct. If we are going to train men for the filthy job of war, we must train them to be utterly unfit for the decent job of civilised living.[22]

The Woman's International League believed that the use of the Black and Tans and Auxiliaries as state terrorist forces against the Irish nationalist movement, and the bulk of the Irish people who supported them, was all part of British Government policy:

Take the most insensitive of the men whom war has calloused, pay them well, feed them highly, do not stint their drinks, keep them confined to barracks in between their licensed outrages. They can then be trusted to pursue that damnable policy of exasperation which, whatever may be Mr George's vacillations, is the policy of those who drive Mr George.[23]

In the ten years after the end of the First World War, pension boards in Britain examined over 100,000 cases of former front line troops suffering from mental disorders. At the start of the Second World War the British government was still paying £2 million a year to shell-shocked veterans of the 1914-1918 war. Wilfred

Owen was killed at the front just before the end of the war. In his poem 'Apologia Pro Poemate Meo' Owen tried to express to the folks back home the feelings of many of the fighting men. The last verse went:

You shall not hear their mirth:
You shall not come to think them well content
By any jest of mine. These men are worth
Your tears. You are not worth their merriment.

Like many soldiers before and since, the Great War veterans were not seeking pity. Instead, they believed they had earned the right to expect the public to understand their situation.

Catch-22

During the Second World War, the war in the air proved a decisive battle ground. Over 57,000 members of Bomber Command were killed and aircrews often sustained 50 per cent casualties on missions. Some faced the statistical odds of zero for surviving a tour of duty. After a number of missions, many crewmen experienced feelings of intense anxiety and depression. Some had nightmares about bombing missions, others would 'freeze' while in the air. Richard Pape, in his book *Boldness Be My Friend*, explained how many crewmen experienced a very real fear that the next mission would be their last:

I strolled back to the mess, coldly, practical, unconcerned. And then it happened. As I walked through the deserted crew room my eye caught the enormous map of Europe on the wall. A terrible feeling of panic gripped me. I stood motionless, staring at the map, my eyes hypnotised by the coloured tapes that indicate the bombing routes. My heart pounded violently; I leaned against the wall gasping and breathless.

To try and pull myself together I began to swear – my infallible cure for nerves. As I steadied blind panic gave way to stark horror. Five words beat into my brain with maddening repetition: 'You will not come back. You will not come back.' I knew then I was doomed.[24]

Sir Arthur Harris, appointed Commander in Chief, Bomber Command, in February 1942, became concerned by the numbers of aircrew reporting sick and asking to be taken off flying duties. He called such men 'weaklings' and 'waverers' and warned his commanders that such men should be dealt with harshly, for 'the risk of contagion is very real'.

In 1988, Simon Berthon produced a documentary, *Whispers in the Air*, for Granada Television. Among former aircrew interviewed was a bomb aimer named Arthur Smith, who began to develop a growing fear of flying. His symptoms increased until on one mission he found himself 'frozen with fear' and unable to carry out his duties. The aircraft returned to base with a 'sick bomb aimer' and he was immediately taken to hospital. When he was found to be physically fit, he was sent to a centre where a psychiatrist interviewed him. It was clearly spelt out to him that if he refused to fly, he would be dealt with harshly, along the lines recommended by Air Chief Marshal Harris.

According to Jack Wallis, a former RAF station adjutant, this meant an immediate reduction in rank to Aircraftsman 2nd class, the lowest rank in the RAF. The 'offender' was posted off station and on his documents 'LMF' (Lack of Moral Fibre) was written in red ink. Arthur Smith was informed that his family, his girlfriend, and his colleagues would be told that he was considered a coward. He was told that in the First World War he would have been charged with 'desertion in the face of the enemy' and shot. Rather than face the degradation, Smith chose to return to flying. The fears continued and a few missions later his aircraft crashed; some of the crew were killed but he survived, albeit with severe burns.

Another aircrew member interviewed was John Wainwright, a rear gunner. On his seventy-second mission his aircraft crashed on landing, injuring him. After recovering in hospital he experienced difficulty in facing a return to flying. Having completed so many missions and been wounded in battle, he thought his removal from combat flying would be an easy process. He recalled that the RAF doctors considered 'I was bonkers, completely bananas, because I didn't want to go over Germany and drop bombs'. Wainwright went through a series of degradations because of his refusal to fly any more.

Sir Arthur Harris ordered that the methods of dealing with cases of 'LMF' be classified as 'top secret'. In 1944, the Secretary of State for Air, Sir

Archibald Sinclair, wrote a private memorandum to Harris to say that if the way the RAF treated its combat fatigue victims were made public, in particular the writing of LMF on their service records, it would be 'indefensible in Parliament'. For a time the documents were marked 'W' for 'waverer' before the insidious practice eventually was ceased.

In 1942, American heavy bombers entered the air war. They were ordered to undertake deep-penetration daylight raids, which the RAF had given up a year before because of the high attrition rate. Within the next two years some 50,000 American aircrew had been killed. While a crew was expected to fly twenty-five missions on a single tour, the average number of missions before death was likely was computed to be only seven. By mid-1943, only one crew in three could expect to complete a tour.

In 1944 it was revealed that hundreds of US bombers had landed in neutral countries such as Sweden and Switzerland. In Sweden most of the aircrews were interned in the village of Falcum. The US Consul in Goteborg, William Cochrane, reported that some cases, where the aircraft was crippled, were genuine – but most were not. From his interviews with internees, Cochrane found that some crews had discussed the option of landing in neutral countries, before flying from their British bases.

A bizarre footnote to this story is provided by Major Urban Drew, a fighter ace whose squadron flew long-range Mustangs to escort the heavy bombers on their missions. Drew recalled a briefing in 1944 at which Mustang pilots were asked to note the markings of any bomber that peeled off formation to head for Switzerland or Sweden. If the bomber seemed to be without battle damage, fighter pilots were to do their best to persuade the defecting crew to return to base. If all else failed, said Major Drew, 'it was understood' that the fighter pilots were to shoot down the defecting aircraft. Drew maintained that this was a clear verbal order and that at squadron level it was not written down because had it appeared in writing it would have been 'unacceptable'.

In the early 1950s Joseph Heller wrote *Catch-22*, a novel about a US air force unit led by a Colonel who kept raising the number of missions his men must fly before returning home, in order that the Pentagon would speed his promotion.

The hero Yossarian approaches the doctor about a fellow pilot:

'Is Orr crazy?'

'He sure is,' Doc Danecka said.

'Can you ground him?'

'I sure can. But first he has to ask me. That's part of the rule.'

'Then why doesn't he ask you to?'

'Because he's crazy,' Doc Danecka said. 'He has to be crazy to keep flying combat missions after the close calls he's had. Sure I can ground Orr. But first he has to ask me to.'

'That's all he has to do to be grounded?'

'That's all. Let him ask me.'

'And then you can ground him?' Yossarian asked.

'No. Then I can't ground him.'

'You mean there's a catch?'

'Sure there's a catch,' Doc Danecka replied. 'Catch-22. Anyone who wants to get out of combat duty isn't really crazy.'

There was only one catch, and that was Catch-22, which specified that a concern for one's own safety in the face of dangers that were real and immediate was the process of a rational mind. Orr was crazy and could be grounded. All he had to do was ask; and as soon as he did, he would no longer be crazy and would have to fly more missions. Orr would be crazy to fly more missions and sane if he didn't, but if he was sane he had to fly them. If he flew them he was crazy and didn't have to; but if he didn't want to he was sane and had to. Yossarian was moved very deeply by the absolute simplicity of this clause of Catch-22 and let out a respectful whistle.

'That's some catch, that Catch-22,' he observed.
'It's the best there is,' Doc Danecka agreed.[25]

While *Catch-22* was fiction, Heller's book expressed the underhand way the authorities dealt with men who had mental problems, forcing them to continue combat duty. The reluctance of both the RAF and US Army Air Force to deal humanely with this issue was not due to a lack of identification of the psychiatric disorders involved. In the combat situation facing them, both Air Chief Marshal Harris and General Henry Arnold, commander of the US Army Air Force, expressed a concern that to allow aircrew suffering from combat fatigue to leave combat operations would be to open up a floodgate: thousands of crewmen would request to be taken off flying duties.

Richard Pape, author of the autobiographical *Boldness Be My Friend*, continued flying till his plane was shot down over Holland. He was badly burned, but evaded the Germans for several months. After capture, he was interrogated by the Gestapo and detained as a prisoner of war. After his death in 1995, an obituarist told how Pape had experienced difficulty settling back into civilian life:

> Like many an-other forced by war to peak too soon, Pape found it hard to settle down to civilian life after his wartime adventures, which won him the Military Medal. He continued to get into trouble of his own making, involving violence or alcohol.
>
> ... He said he wrote his first book to exorcise the 'demons' which plagued him after the war. It appeared in 1953. In that year he was fined for firing shots outside the home of his estranged first wife. Boldness was turning into an enemy.
>
> ... The second of his 12 books described ... [how] ... he was also charged with drunken driving. He told the court he had been upset by a radio dramatisation of *Boldness* and was acquitted. Two years later he was acquitted again on a similar charge. His second wife left him in 1961, accusing him of physical cruelty. A 'heroic' drinker, Pape was given to chasing his literary agent round the office with a sword stick.
>
> Another drunken driving charge in Papua New Guinea in 1965 was

dismissed after evidence that Pape had hallucinated at the scene, thinking he was trapped in a burning plane and that the police were the Gestapo. He offered to drink a bottle of whisky in court to prove he could handle drink.[26]

Combat Fatigue

In the early phases of the Second World War, the military establishment was concerned that 23 per cent of casualties evacuated from the war zone were soldiers diagnosed as suffering from psychiatric disorders. Resources were allocated to provide on-the-spot treatment, which aimed to put all but the worst cases back into combat as soon as possible. Subsequently, during the Normandy landings, two centres for 'exhausted' troops were opened on the beachheads.

Frontline treatment for psychiatric problems, or 'combat fatigue' as it became known, was a great success from the point of view of the military command. The proportion of soldiers suffering from combat fatigue who were evacuated from the front line was reduced to 6 per cent; the rest received immediate treatment and were returned to the battle zone. A study of some thousands of American combat casualties during the Normandy landings concluded: 'all normal men will eventually suffer combat exhaustion in prolonged, continuous and severe combat. The exception to this rule are psychotic [insane] soldiers, and a number of examples of this have been observed.'[27]

Some of the worst cases from the beachhead centres were evacuated to hospitals in England and found themselves sharing wards with survivors from the London Blitz. Common symptoms were noted between these patients. Some stammered or lost speech altogether, while others spoke in a staccato fashion. Some collapsed, writhing and jerking in an uncoordinated yet regular manner. Most appeared to be in a state of exhaustion, sometimes descending into stupors.

Increasing attention was paid to psychiatric problems associated with combat situations by military and medical establishments. By 1954, a search of medical literature showed 1,166 articles on the subject of combat fatigue. There were varied and conflicting theories as to the cause, nature and treatment of this condition, but most of the experts seemed to agree that the disorder was 'transient'. This concept fitted in well with the system of dealing with these problems at the front: instant treatment and a rapid return to combat (just like the system adopted by the British military authorities for the physically injured in the First World War). But evidence was accumulating that experience of war might produce long-term psychological effects in some veterans:

> Now there are mutilations, midst absurdity and evil, in any war. Men who fight wars inevitably become aware of the terrible disparity between romantic views of heroism expressed 'back home' and the reality of degradation and unspeakable suffering they have witnessed, experienced, and caused. One thinks of the answer given by Audie Murphy, much-decorated hero of World War II, to the question put to him about how long it takes a man to get over his war experiences. Murphy's reply, recorded in his obituary, was that one never does.[28]

The US military authorities in the Second World War showed increased concern about the problems of combat fatigue among their soldiers. At times during conflict, over 50 per cent of battlefield casualties had been psychological in nature. Psychiatric doctors began to appear at the front, and the 'exhaustion centres' introduced during the Normandy landings were adopted for all battle zones. Only the most hopeless cases were evacuated.

In later wars, the desire to drastically reduce 'combat fatigue' evacuees led to an even greater emphasis on the military management of soldiers suffering from mental disorders. Whilst on-site treatment increased military efficiency by keeping greater numbers of soldiers in combat, it is open to question whether this benefited soldiers suffering from psychiatric problems. The cycle of combat-disorder-treatment-combat, sometimes occurring over and over again, risked creation of long-term psychiatric problems.

Most experts still considered the problem to be transient however, so long-term effects were not even thought possible. But subsequent studies of Second World War veterans showed that those who had suffered combat fatigue and others with no previous history of this condition were starting to describe common problems. These included: feelings of intense anxiety, depression, nightmares about battle experiences, problems with family relationships, displaying aggressive behaviour and getting into fights. Post-traumatic stress disorders were, at last, beginning to be recorded and examined.

After the two world wars, the home population welcomed back those who had fought overseas. Many of those returning veterans never really got over their experiences. A few appeared demented, shuffling around the streets. Neighbours would good-naturedly tap one finger to their heads. 'He was in the war, you know,' they would say by way of explanation. Other veterans showed no outward sign, but were unable to settle down. Many found solace in drink, some drifted into crime and violence.

Vietnam

It was the involvement of the USA in Vietnam that most awakened people to the severe psychological problems that wars can bring to those that fight them. The US military planners had taken into account the possibility of psychiatric casualties. Fighting men were sent to the war zone for a set time; one year for most soldiers and 13 months for marines. Each man knew he would leave after this period, and this encouraged soldiers to 'hold on', to keep going and see it out.

A medical apparatus was put in place to deal with psychological casualties as close as possible to the combat zone. The aim was to return patients back as quickly as possible to their unit and the front line. Drugs were often used as part of the treatment. In Vietnam, the percentage of US combatants who had to be evacuated because of psychiatric breakdown was under 2 per cent. The US military planners thought they had reduced the problem to an almost irrelevant level.

It was only after many of the troops had returned to the USA that problems began to surface. Back home, many Vietnam veterans felt alienated and isolated and had difficulty settling down. They flew into rages with little or no provocation, often using violence against their partners and children or others around them. Many chose to live a solitary life, usually heavily armed, in the national parks or other wild countryside. *Taxi Driver* was one of many films that portrayed violent Vietnam veterans; ironically, *First Blood*, the first Rambo book, was written about just such a character:

With America splitting apart because of Vietnam, maybe it was time to write a novel that dramatised the philosophical division in our society, that showed the brutality of war right under our noses. I decided my catalytic character would be a Vietnam veteran, a Green Beret who, after many harrowing missions, had been captured by the enemy, escaped, and returned home to be given America's highest distinction, the Congressional Medal of Honour. But he would bring something back with him from Southeast Asia, what we now call posttrauma stress syndrome. Haunted by nightmares about what he had done in the war, embittered by civilian indifference and sometimes hostility towards the sacrifice he had made for his country, he would drop out of society to wander the backroads of the nation he loved.[29]

Vietnam proved to be an unpopular and ultimately, from the US establishment's point of view, an unsuccessful war. In this case there was no ticker-tape parade to welcome back victorious troops. The fixed term of combat was found to be something of a Trojan horse. Soldiers, replaced after they had completed their tour of duty, returned as individuals to an indifferent or even hostile home population just a jet flight away. Having seen their combat period through, sometimes after treatment for psychiatric problems, some returnees found their memories of the war, combined with the gap between their expectations and the reality of the situation on their return, overwhelming. Just over 58,000 Americans were killed in Vietnam. Back in the USA, 110,000 Vietnam veterans have died from 'war-related' problems. Over 60,000 of these deaths were suicides. One Vietnam veteran stated after his tour of duty:

> They gave me a Bronze Star ... and they put me up for a Silver Star. But I said you can shove it up your ass. ... I threw all the others away. The only thing I kept was the Purple Heart because I still think I was wounded.[30]

In 1980, five years after the ending of the Vietnam war, Post-traumatic Stress Disorder was officially recognised as a condition when it was included in the third edition of the *Diagnostic and Statistical Manual of the American Psychiatric Association (DSMIII)*. It had taken a lengthy campaign by Vietnam veterans and their friends to persuade the US government to admit that some returning soldiers were suffering from PTSD and other rehabilitation problems.

DSMIII described PTSD as the 'Experiencing of a certain set of symptoms following a psychologically traumatic event that is generally outside the range of usual human experience'. The *Viet Vet – Survival Guide* explained that 'A vet with PTSD generally has one or more combinations of symptoms', adding that these varied from vet to vet, it listed some of these symptoms:

☐ A psychological numbness, usually directly after the event, and continuing for weeks, months, or even years.

☐ Guilt over surviving when others did not.

☐ Anxiety or nervousness.

☐ Depression or deep sadness.

☐ Nightmares or flashbacks in which the veteran reexperiences the traumatic event.

☐ Jumpiness, especially in response to sounds that remind the veteran of the event or of the war in general.

☐ Difficulty developing close relationships with people at work, at home, or in social settings.

☐ Difficulty sleeping.

☐ Difficulty concentrating.

☐ Avoidance of certain memories.

☐ Attempts to calm down by using alcohol or drugs.[31]

The war caused deep divisions within the USA, and many Vietnam veterans, and consequently those who came into contact with them, are still suffering from that war:

During the last decade of the twentieth century, America is still haunted by Vietnam. In 1990, a definitive study of the Vietnam generation revealed astonishing psychological costs of the war, still affecting veterans themselves and reverberating throughout much of American society 15 years after the last American combatant had left Vietnam. The study found that 15.2 percent of all male Vietnam theater veterans, 497,000 of the 3.14 million men who served there, currently suffer from posttraumatic stress disorder.... those with posttraumatic stress disorder are prone to other profound affects: they frequently experience various psychiatric illnesses; they are five times

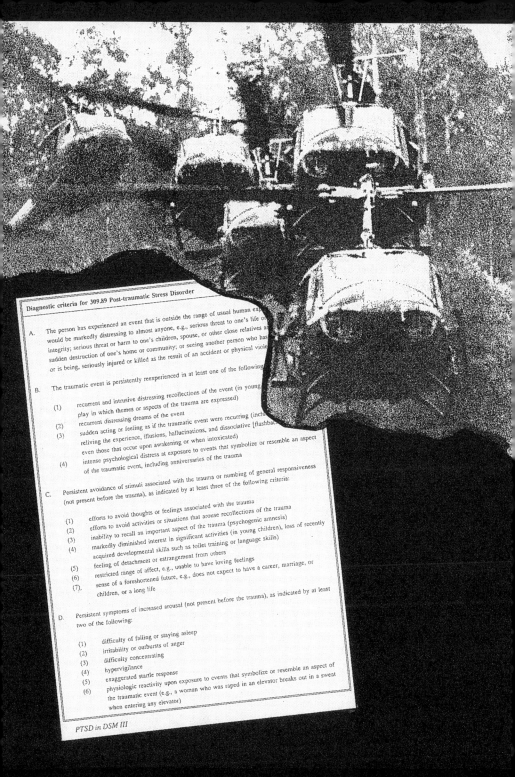

Diagnostic criteria for 309.89 Post-traumatic Stress Disorder

A. The person has experienced an event that is outside the range of usual human exp
   would be markedly distressing to almost anyone, e.g., serious threat to one's life or
   integrity; serious threat or harm to one's children, spouse, or other close relatives an
   sudden destruction of one's home or community; or seeing another person who has
   or is being, seriously injured or killed as the result of an accident or physical viole

B. The traumatic event is persistently reexperienced in at least one of the following

   (1)   recurrent and intrusive distressing recollections of the event (in young
         play in which themes or aspects of the trauma are expressed)
   (2)   recurrent distressing dreams of the event
   (3)   sudden acting or feeling as if the traumatic event were recurring (inclu
         reliving the experience, illusions, hallucinations, and dissociative [flashbac
         even those that occur upon awakening or when intoxicated)
   (4)   intense psychological distress at exposure to events that symbolize or resemble an aspect
         of the traumatic event, including anniversaries of the trauma

C. Persistent avoidance of stimuli associated with the trauma or numbing of general responsiveness
   (not present before the trauma), as indicated by at least three of the following criteria:

   (1)   efforts to avoid thoughts or feelings associated with the trauma
   (2)   efforts to avoid activities or situations that arouse recollections of the trauma
   (3)   inability to recall an important aspect of the trauma (psychogenic amnesia)
   (4)   markedly diminished interest in significant activities (in young children), loss of recently
         acquired developmental skills such as toilet training or language skills)
   (5)   feeling of detachment or estrangement from others
   (6)   restricted range of affect, e.g., unable to have loving feelings
   (7). sense of a foreshortened future, e.g., does not expect to have a career, marriage, or
         children, or a long life

D. Persistent symptoms of increased arousal (not present before the trauma), as indicated by at least
   two of the following:

   (1)   difficulty of falling or staying asleep
   (2)   irritability or outbursts of anger
   (3)   difficulty concentrating
   (4)   hypervigilance
   (5)   exaggerated startle response
   (6)   physiologic reactivity upon exposure to events that symbolize or resemble an aspect of
         the traumatic event (e.g., a woman who was raped in an elevator breaks out in a sweat
         when entering any elevator)

PTSD in DSM III

WHAT IT'S REALLY LIKE
TO BE A SOLDIER IN ULSTER

A LOUD noise or a car backfiring still makes Bobby Robertson jump and cringe.

It is a life-saving habit he picked up in Northern Ireland and can't lose.

He accepts it, doesn't apologise for it, and understands it better than any civilian who doesn't know the pressures of patrolling a Belfast street.

Bobby Robertson was a corporal in the Black Watch until last December. He is out now, and lives in a council house in Leven, Fife. But during his nine years of service he had six tours in the torn province.

He read the news yesterday that a 20-year-old trooper who had gone berserk with a rifle had been shot dead by Army friends.

"It's tragic. But I am surprised it hasn't happened before. The tensions over there are unbeliev

MATES SHOOT MAD SOLDIER

From the editions of yesterday's Daily Record

TORMENTED squaddies Jim Scott and Timothy Haslin gave themselves up yesterday.

The pair, who went on the run four days after finishing their first tour in Northern Ireland, surrendered themselves to military police at Edinburgh Castle first thing.

The Royal Scots pair went AWOL hours before their pal Lawrence Dickson – killed by an IRA sniper – was buried.

HELP

In an exclusive interview in yesterday's Daily Record, the scared squaddies said: "We just can't go back to Ulster.

"We are literally cracking up with the strain."

The pair, from West Lothian, told how they stared death in the face every day.

The Se

Ulster fear squaddies surrender at castle

Falklands veterans 'still suffering war trauma'

Chris Mihill
Medical Correspondent

SERVICEMEN who fought the Falklands may be suffering from psychic problems, 10 years after the conflict, a specialist warns in a study published today.

Roderick Orner, clinical psychologist at Lincoln county hospital, who has studied post-traumatic stress disorder (PTSD) among Falklands veterans, says Ministry of Defence efforts to help servicemen have been inadequate, and there is no network of support for those no longer in the services.

His study, carried out between 1986 and 1989, found that 63 per cent of 53 Falklands veterans who left the services were suffering problems such as flashbacks, re-experiencing what happened to them in the war, feelings of panic in crowds, hyper-arousal, sleeplessness, memory difficulties, emotional withdrawal and difficulties with relationships.

He found that the course of chronic PTSD usually fluctuates but gets gradually worse. The 10th anniversary next week of the end of the conflict would bring back powerful feelings of loss for many Falklands servicemen.

Mr Orner recommends a long-term follow-up survey of those involved in war, "incorporating treatment evaluations and welfare rights campaigns."

...SECOND ... MAN WHO HAD ... EVERYTHING

Killer guilty of jail murder

By KEN SMITH and
DANI GARAVELLI

CONVICTED killer Anthony McCullagh had already committed a brutal murder when he stabbed a fellow prisoner to death.

Today he is beginning a second life sentence for the murder of prisoner Kenneth Seaman committed just three years after he was sentenced for killing a defenceless teenager.

The killings were startlingly similar. Each victim was stabbed several times before being left to die by "the man who hated everything".

McCullagh, whose parents live in Ashington, denied murdering multiple rapist Seaman but judge Mr Justice Waite described it as "a deliberate and unprovoked" killing.

He said he had read his letter of remorse and medical reports and considered him a man

incapable of controlling anger.

McCullagh, originally of Chester-le-Street, was jailed three years ago when he stabbed 18-year-old John Collins to death in a school playground in Birmingham.

It was a motiveless attack. Mr Collins, a metal worker, died in hospital three hours later. He had been stabbed five times.

At his trial for the Collins killing, McCullagh— a former soldier with the Royal Transport Corps, Aldershot — was described as "a man who hated everything."

He told Birmingham Crown Court: "When I saw that boy in the street I just had to do him damage."

... Thomas Gow ... in a bad way ... into a bit ... for the other party ... a court was told yesterday.

He began to shout and swear, smashed a window and punched a woman, breaking her nose.

Inverness Sheriff Court heard Gow, 23, was one of a group of Ardersier-based Royal Scots invited to a party in Nairn.

Aileen Mac...

The Army's knife fight

BRITISH soldiers are smuggling illegal flick-knives into the country, it was admitted yesterday.

And an officer said that the Army had a

having an offensive weapon – a flick-knife in the door pocket of car when he was stopped routinely by police at Aviemore.

Cairney, of the Royal Logistics Corps, claimed that the knife was nev more likely than those without the disorder to be unemployed; 70 percent have been divorced; almost half have been arrested or in jail at least once; and they are two to six times as likely to abuse alcohol or drugs.[32]

Most veterans of the Second World War experienced situations of great violence. However, nearly everyone at home supported the fighting. This recognition of a 'just war' allowed veterans to come to terms with the horrors they had witnessed and been a part of:

> Veterans have always come to some terms with their war experiences through some formulation of their survival that permits them to overcome much of their death anxiety and death guilt. ... Crucial even to this partial resolution of survivor conflict is the veteran's capacity to believe that his war had purpose and significance beyond the immediate horrors he witnessed. He can then connect his own actions with ultimate humane principles, and can come to feel that he had performed a dirty but necessary job.[33]

In conflicts like Vietnam the conventional rules of warfare tend to be thrown out of the window and the concepts of justified war start to break down. Wars are usually fought in a onslaught of propaganda and a crescendo of patriotism. Vietnam was no different, except that conflicts like this are often not declared as wars, and subsequently patriotism and propaganda take more subtle and hidden forms. Returning Vietnam veterans often found that the home population had a simplistic view of the war that was far from most GI's experiences. In many soldiers' minds, Vietnam could never be a good or honourable war:

> ... the central fact of the Vietnam War is that no one really believes in it. The larger purposes put forth to explain the American presence – repelling outside invaders, or giving the people of the South an opportunity to choose their own form of government – are directly contradicted by the overwhelming evidence a GI encounters that he is the outside invader, that the government he has come to defend is justly hated by the people he has come to help, and that he, the American helper, is hated by them most of all.[34]

The contradictions between the indoctrination given to the troops, coupled to the propaganda justifying the war, and the GI's own experiences at the front, led to doubts growing in the minds of the soldiers. Many GIs adopted a cynical and nihilistic attitude towards the war. Back home, veterans were told to forget about the conflict, but many found that impossible to do. Jan Barry, former president of Vietnam Veterans Against the War, wrote the poem *Viet Nam*:

> Once you were a strange, alien name...
>
> then you were a small, damp green
>
> hostile land
>
> where ... I ... nearly died
>
>
> Now you are ... a part of me

Towards the end of the First World War it was the realisation of what the conflict was doing to the soldiers that started to turn the British public against the war. In the USA it was the realisation of what the Vietnam war was doing to so many of the GIs, plus the active opposition to the war by many Vietnam veterans, that hastened US withdrawal. The true story of My Lai and other atrocities came out and were believed by the people of the USA, when Vietnam veterans spoke out about the war.

Britain's Colonial Wars

During the 1966/67 soccer season, in football grounds up and down England, gangs of youths used the following jingle to taunt the police who faced them on the terraces:

> Harry Roberts – he's our man,
>
> He shoots cops – bang, bang, bang.

On a sunny afternoon, two weeks after England had won the football World Cup, three policemen were shot dead on a west London street, just a few miles from Wembley Stadium. Two men were quickly arrested and a search was undertaken for the third man, who was known to have started the shooting and killed two of the policemen.

After a three-month manhunt, described as the biggest ever launched in Britain, the third man, Harry Roberts, was caught hiding in a wood near Bishop's

Stortford. He had been living rough in a camouflaged hide made of wood and plastic bags.

Roberts had always been a bit of a tearaway. He had left school early, already having a conviction for handling stolen goods. He then went from job to job before his call-up for National Service; 'He then joined the Rifle Brigade, becoming a marksman and a lance corporal and served in Malaya during the emergency; jungle training and guerrilla warfare taught him much and hardened him.'[35] Harry Roberts also served in Kenya. His wife Margaret later said that after he was demobbed, 'He seemed bitter, and talked about killing and the fear of battle and the danger. ... He seemed to have become slightly ruthless and much more tough.'[36]

Roberts' conditioning reflected the ruthlessness of the colonial wars he had been part of. In 1952, a speech by Gerald Templer, the British High Commissioner of Malaya, had been broadcast in Australia. Templer told his radio audience, 'the hard core of communists in this country are fanatics and must be, and will be, exterminated'.[37] In Malaya, army units kept score-boards of CTs (communist terrorists) killed. A National Serviceman described how units who had killed 'CTs' used to bring the bodies back for identification. When that proved difficult, they brought back the heads only:

> As Private Houchin walked past me, I noticed he was carrying a large, round object, wrapped in a poncho, on his back. He usually had a ready smile, but this time he looked a bit grim and, when I asked him what he was carrying, he just said, 'A head.' I couldn't believe it, so he explained.
>
> It seems that the bodies were proving so difficult to carry that the lieutenant had ordered the Ibans to chop the heads off, so that just the heads could be brought out of the jungle as evidence. The Ibans ... had refused this grisly task, so the lieutenant had ordered some of his men to do it. Poor Private Houchin seemed full up with emotion, so I went to have a word with Lieutenant Surtees.
>
> When I got near to Surtees, I saw that the other lieutenant was with him, and they seemed to be discussing the very issue ... so I just hung around within earshot. ... I heard Surtees tell him that such actions would give the

men nervous breakdowns. As far as Houchin was concerned he was right, for he was the man who was to cry out in his sleep.[38]

In his book, *The Malayan Emergency*, Robert Jackson quoted a young British officer who had been involved in the fighting; 'We were shooting people. We were killing them. ... This was raw savage success. It was butchery. It was horror.' Many of the soldiers were National Servicemen, but Jackson said, 'like seasoned jungle veterans, they became accustomed to it. They coped, and coped very well, and boys of nineteen emerged from the jungle as men with leadership experience that would carry them through any experience they might encounter on their return to civilian life.'[39] Harry Roberts and the relatives of the three dead policemen might have disagreed. In early 1993, after serving twenty-six years of a life sentence, the news leaked out that Roberts was being considered for parole. Police groups said Roberts should never be released and the *Guardian* journalist Nick Davies visited him in Dartmoor prison. Harry Roberts told Davies about the police shootings:

> We were professional criminals. We don't react the same same way as ordinary people. The police aren't like real people to us. They're strangers, they're the enemy. And you don't feel remorse for killing a stranger. I do feel sorry for what we did to their families. I do. But it's like people I killed in Malaya when I was in the army. You don't feel remorse.[40]

By the end of 1974 police in the Midlands and the north of England were chasing a robber who had carried out a series of raids on post offices. The descriptions of the mystery man were always the same: army camouflage suit, black plimsolls, white gloves and, covering his face, a black hood, across which a visor-like slash had been cut for eye holes. Nicknamed the Black Panther, the man was always armed with a pistol and a sawn-off shotgun. The robberies had netted him some £20,000, but he had left three men dead and others badly injured.

In early 1975, the Black Panther committed the crime that would bring him nationwide notoriety. He kidnapped seventeen-year-old Lesley Whittle, intending to ransom her for £50,000. But his victim met a horrible death. Lesley Whittle's body was found, tied up and naked, in the ventilating area of a sewer system. Around her neck was a noose of wire with which her kidnapper had secured her to an iron ladder. A huge manhunt was launched, but it was not until the end of 1975 that the Black Panther, Donald Neilson, was unmasked and captured.

Neilson had been born in Morley, near Bradford, in 1936. Originally, his surname had been Nappy, but after being taunted at school as 'Dirty Nappy', he changed his name in later life to Neilson. A neighbour said Neilson was 'Rather secretive. ... He looked every inch a part-time paratrooper. We called him "Castro" because he always wore battledress and marched down the street.'[41]

In early 1955, Neilson, then nineteen years old, was called up for National Service. For most of his time in the army he was involved in colonial conflicts:

> His two years in the Army shaped his life, giving him interests and
> excitements unknown before: the peculiar pleasure of jungle warfare and
> survival skills, of the power of weapons, of fitness and self-reliance. He
> relished the hide-and-seek thrills of security patrols, dealing with Mau Mau
> gangs on Mount Kenya, EOKA guerrillas in Cyprus, and Arab nationalists
> in Aden. A soldier in Kenya said: 'After Morley it was a bit like paradise. The
> sun was always shining. ... I wouldn't look any further than Kenya to work
> out how Nappy [Neilson] learned the tricks of his trade ... In a way it's not
> surprising that one of our number used his training for illegal purposes in
> later life.'[42]

All countries who sent men to fight in foreign wars experienced difficulties with some of their returning troops. Colonial conflicts, especially, were usually dirty and brutal affairs, often morally corrupting for those caught up in them. Most National Servicemen sent to Kenya experienced killings, like these soldiers who found a hut in a 'prohibited area' and waited in ambush inside:

> ... as the Mau Mau bent over to come in, [we] opened up with the Bren
> gun. The weight of the bullets pushed the Mau Mau back; but when [we]
> stopped firing, of course, with the momentum, the Mau Mau started to
> come in again. So [we] shot him again. When we saw him the next morning,
> oh God! he was shot to pieces; but ... [we] could still hear him moaning out
> there after [we'd] actually shot him. The corporal said to the rifleman to go

out and finish him off. This little lad, a Londoner, he ... went out there and put the actual muzzle of the rifle on his forehead and pulled the trigger; but the next morning ... we saw he'd actually shot him in the throat, he was shaking so much. He would have been dead, anyway; he had his kidneys hanging out – you imagine, half a magazine of Bren.

... in the Aberdare Forest you were allowed to shoot any black man – if he's black, you shoot him because he's Mau Mau – it was a prohibited area.[43]

Neilson said about his period in the King's Own Yorkshire Light Infantry; 'I enjoyed my time in the Army. But I never admitted owt about it. ... It's possible to be afraid and at the same time to enjoy oneself'.[44] Neilson was to find his later life dominated by his brutalising army experiences:

... He spent six months in Kenya altogether. Those six months probably had a greater influence on what was to become of him than any other period of his life. They began with an intensive period of jungle warfare training, when he was taught how to fight with the rubber-stocked, short-barrelled .303 jungle rifle British troops in Kenya were issued with, and which bear a striking resemblance to sawn-off shotguns, and how to operate as a completely independent unit.

The tactics of the British were to cut off the terrorist supplies of food by preventing them from reaching the lowland farms of the white settlers which had been their main source of supply hitherto, and to harass and harry them in the forests.

... Nappy [Neilson] learned racialism and there were apparently other lessons to be learned too.

... Few national servicemen can have served in so many trouble spots as Nappy [Neilson] did in his two years with the Queen, or seen so much action. It was perhaps an experience he never really recovered from.[45]

Ex-soldier and colonial war veteran Donald Neilson received life sentences for each of four murders, plus 61 years for kidnapping. A decade before, the *Daily Mail* had expressed its outrage at the shooting of the three policemen in west London:

In Britain the policeman is still the walking sign which says that a society has reached and takes for granted a certain stable normality of public order and decency ... That is why the death of a policeman by violence is felt so deeply by us all. The deaths of the three men at Shepherd's Bush, senselessly and deliberately gunned down on the job of maintaining that order and decency, come as a frightful shock that seems to rock the very earth. A dazed incredulity is followed by the realisation that order is not to be taken for granted. The jungle is still there. There are still wild beasts in it to be controlled.[46]

In fact, the actual connection with the jungle was that it was there – in Malaya and Kenya – that Harry Roberts had learned to kill for Queen and country. That fateful day in Shepherd's Bush the relatively civilised face of law and order at home, in the form of the unarmed London bobby, had met the uncivilised face of British colonial law and order, in the form of ex-soldier Harry Roberts. Brutalised by his experiences in Malaya and Kenya, Roberts had brought home those wars. The result was three dead policemen. But Roberts and Neilson were not the only young men called up for National Service, trained and indoctrinated for combat against 'terrorists' and then thrust into the middle of colonial conflicts. After service in Britain's colonial wars, few veterans were debriefed or received any preparation for re-entry back into civilian life.

Aden and Northern Ireland

Towards the end of the 1970s, Britain was horrified by a series of brutal murders of young women, many picked up from 'red light' areas in northern cities. Reading about the latest 'Yorkshire Ripper' murder in 1978 had a profound effect on one Scottish ex-soldier. The lurid accounts of the multiple stabbings of the latest victim evoked memories of a night six years before when he had been a member of an army patrol in Northern Ireland.

In October 1972 two young Catholics, Andrew Murray and Michael Naan, had been found killed at isolated farm buildings in County Fermanagh. A pitchfork was thought to have been the murder weapon; one victim had been stabbed seventeen times, and the other thirteen times, through the heart and chest. A sectarian motive was suspected for the killings, and loyalists were thought to be the likely perpetrators of the crime that became known as the 'pitch-fork murders'.

The ex-soldier knew who had really carried out those killings in County Fermanagh and the similarity between them and the 'Yorkshire Ripper' murders began to prey on his mind. Convinced that the killings must have been carried out by the same people, he went to the police and gave them full details of the killings in Ireland.

In reality there was no link between the two crimes. But the British police were under intense public pressure to catch the 'Yorkshire Ripper', so they began to investigate the allegations. In 1980, two of the ex-squaddie's former fellow soldiers, sergeants Stanley Hathaway and John Byrne, were tried and jailed for life for the murder of the two farm-workers. When Hathaway confessed to the police, he burst into tears and said, 'I suppose I have been trying to put it out of my mind. I did it. I did the killings. I killed them and they just wouldn't stop screaming. Oh my God. I have been having nightmares about it.'[47] Other members of the patrol, including the officer in charge, Lieutenant Snowball, received lesser sentences for aiding and abetting or withholding information.

It emerged during the trial that the murder weapon was not a pitchfork as first thought. The stabbings were in fact carried out with a bowie knife which one of the soldiers possessed. Many soldiers in Ireland carry 'personal weapons' to which those in authority turn a blind eye.

The story did not end there. The ex-soldier received several death threats during the trial, which he believed had come from members of his former unit. Angry and upset, he handed over to the Scottish *Sunday Mail* a dossier containing information on up to forty killings carried out by fellow soldiers in Aden fourteen years previously.

A few of these were printed by the newspaper in early 1981 and a controversy ensued, with the *Sunday Mail* being inundated with letters. Some, from serving soldiers, complained bitterly about former mates telling tales out of school, and attacked the paper for printing material detrimental to the honour of the regiment. Others, mainly ex-soldiers, wrote in telling how the terrible events in Aden had been on their minds. Unable to forget, they welcomed the opportu-

Soldiers jailed for farm killings

RIPPER TIP-OFF SOLVES CRIME

THE CRUCIAL clue which led to the conviction in a Belfast Court yesterday of members of a British army regiment who were found guilty of murdering two Co. Fermanagh men in a savage knifing attack on an isolated farm in 1972 came from a former member of the regiment who was horrified by a killing attributed to the Yorkshire Ripper.

Army sergeants get life for Ulster killings

From David Beresford in Belfast.

TWO soldiers in Belfast yesterday were sentenced to life imprisonment for murdering

The trial of the four soldiers came to an unexpectedly abrupt conclusion last night after they had changed their pleas.

the amended plea of manslaughter.

Mr Justice McDermot, who took less than 20 minutes to

brought grief on their families, and it was also sad and tragic for their regiment.

He added : "In the

Fermanagh farm of Michael Naan, aged 31, to interrogate him about alleged IRA

then killed Andrew Murray, Mr Naan's friend who had witnessed the incident, fearing he would give evidence against them.

An Army officer, Captain Andrew Snowball, aged 28, who had sent the patrol out, was told of the killings but decided to try to cover it up "for the good of the Army and the regiment."

The four-day trial was marked by repeated adjournments because Sgt Hathaway was breaking down. At one

Turn to back page, col. 1

I shot them because they were Arabs

AN ex-Argyll and Sutherland Highlander has confessed to shooting unarmed innocent civilians in Aden.

And he has claimed that Arabs were murdered out of hand during the Argylls' six-month tour of duty there in 1967.

In a signed statement made to the Sunday Mail, the soldier alleged that cold-blooded killings were frequent and were condoned by some Scots officers.

The killings, he claimed, started almost immediately after the massacre of 12 soldiers—including three Argylls—outside the police barracks in Crater.

After the ambush, the mutilated bodies were brought back to the Argylls' HQ. Officers, he says, made it clear they wanted revenge.

The ex-Argyll told the Mail: "I saw some of our soldiers' bodies which had missing limbs and other damage. Because of this, anger ran very highly among the Argylls.

"Some officers made their feelings clear. They said we should get the bastards back when we got into Crater. We were told to expect a lot of opposition and we were very surprised when there was so little.

Unarmed

"My platoon went into an official building. There were about five of us. "Three locals were seated at a table in one of the rooms. No warnings were given.

"They were shot where they sat. We all shot them because they were Arabs. There were never other killings."

The ex-Argyll who says he regrets the killings went on: "During my service there I shot a further two Arabs. Both were in the street, and we had been told to shoot anyone who was acting suspiciously or ran away.

"These men were unarmed,

although they were running away from me. Given the chance, all the soldiers I knew did the same thing.

"Some officers made it clear that no questions would be asked. I was never asked to sign any report about the deaths.

driving along the main road road blocks were left open to let through.

"Two Arabs who passed the blocks were shot, but they not even been asked to stop.

"Some prisoners were taken intelligence section, or to the inspection centre.

"I was sometimes given the ... of the dead

WHAT THREE OTHE

Our guns riddled a shanty town

THE night a Crater shanty town was raked by machine-gun fire was witnessed by one soldier.

The ex-Argyll said: "One patrol had suffered a grenade attack. Some of our boys were slightly wounded.

"Immediately we took up positions and watched a searchlight scan the shanty town.

"Wherever the searchlight beam fell a machine-gun—using heavy vehicle bullets—fired a 20 to 30 round burst.

"The homes where men, women and children lived provided scant protection from the bullets.

"Three other searchlights and machine-gun posts did the same thing on other sections of the town.

officers whom he claims were involved in indiscriminate killings.

"I witnessed two separate occasions when Arab cars were

- "Soldiers told me how they beat up civilians they found after curfew.

"And they showed me some of their booty—radios and clothes stolen from their victims.

Thefts

"A lot of soldiers made money by robbing civilians during searches done at gunpoint.

"I heard that businessmen fleeing the Crater had money belts or wallets removed and their cash stolen.

"It was a well-known fact in the Crater that guys on search duty could make lots of dough. I reckon that during the occupation these thefts amounted to thousands of pounds."

THE ADEN FILE

They killed for more golliwog labels

ANOTHER former Argyll soldier has come forward with further disclosures of alleged atrocities committed by his regiment in Aden.

The soldier, a private in the party which took the Crater district of 1967, said he was sickened by the "unnecessary violence" used by the Jocks.

He spoke of the inter-platoon rivalry which

existed for Robertson Jam Golliwog stickers, awarded by an officer to any Argyll who notched up the killing of an Arab.

He said: "At one stage, my platoon had notched up 13 kills and another platoon were one kill behind.

"The Corporal even told the Private he was to use his bayonet, for it was to be that kind of killing.

"They went into an alley and killed a young Arab who was out after curfew."

Getting drugs was easy.. the Army is like an opium den

Gulf war vet caught with kilo of dope escapes jail

A FORMER soldier yesterday told of drinking and drugs ... inside an Army PRISON.

Young Peter Flanagan was sent to the glasshouse after going AWOL because of bullying.

And yesterday, as he revealed he planned to sue the Army, he claimed: "The Army is just like one big opium den."

BULLIES M EAT RAB

How the Recor

RUN

Peter, 18, went on the run from the largely-Scottish 40 Field Regiment of the Royal Artillery in October last year.

Whileon therun, the teenager, from Chapelhall, Lanarkshire, told the Record how he was persistently bullied.

After seven weekson the run, Peter turned

EXCLUSIVE
By DAVID THOMPSON

beer and whisky.

GULF War veteran caught with £8000 worth of drugs walked free from a yesterday.

Judge said he was taking into account ne Anderson's exemplary Army record.

Johnston told the first offender: "I don't see vice to your ould not be as a factor to

n raided Anderson's in Adelaide Street, ngston, West Lothian, March.

hey had received a tip and found a kilo of abis resin.

employed Anderson detectives: "I was to watch them. I am ealer."

Stash

igh Court in heard that the claimed he had stash the drugs eylender to whom d £200.

nderson, 29, who admit- being concerned in the supply of drugs, agreed to do it on the basis the debt would be wiped out.

Alan Muir, defending said that after a was discharged."

By GORDON McILWRAITH

Royal Scots regiment, he borrowed the cash to buy Christmas presents for his youngson.

But when he failed to pay it back he was told: "Watch the stuff or see what happens."

Mr Muir added that during the Gulf War campaign Anderson was injured when an ammunition box exploded.

And, while serving in Northern Ireland, a friend was shot during a patrol in South Armagh.

After leaving the forces with an exemplary record, he was treated for depression and anxiety.

Deferring sentence for 12 months, Lord Johnson warned Anderson: " strongly advise you to keep ouble and get on the sentence.

Crackdown on army drug use

Army officers and soldiers were last night given official warning of random drug tests to combat soaring abuse. Tests will start in 28 days to give abusers a chance to give up. Convictions have rocketed to more than 420 a year, compared with 88 in 1988 and only 30 a year in the RAF.

Drug troops face sack

MOST of the 22 Scots squaddies caught in random drug tests last week are likely to be sacked.

The soldiers tested positive for cannabis, Ecstasy and speed in the swoop on the Argyll and Sutherland Highlanders at their Edinburgh

SUN, Thur

18 SOLDIERS HELD IN NIGHTCLUB DRUG SCANDAL

Sheriff jails drugs Marine

A MARINE who supplied LSD to friends at a rave was jailed for nine months yesterday.

Marcus Stewart's six-year military career now lies in ruins as a result of the sentence.

By BRANDON MALINSKY

EIGHTEEN soldiers serving in Northern Ireland face the boot after testing positive for drugs.

Military police swooped on their base after a tip that squaddies and NCOs had been taking Ecstasy in a nightclub.

The 18 are all from the First Battalion, The Royal Regiment of Wales where Prince Charles is Colonel-in-Chief. Last night they were confined to barracks. The

EXCLUSIVE

Army's Special Investigation Branch carried out tests on a number of men earlier this week. An initial "field test", believed to be a blood sample, proved positive on the 18.

A second set of formal tests were then carried out. Urine samples from these have been sent away to a laboratory for more detailed analysis.

Most of the 18 — regimental motto Gwell angau ns Chywilydd (Death Before Dishonour)— are squaddies. The others are junior non

commissioned officers. If the second tests prove positive, they could be discharged.

An Army source said: "Drug-taking in the Army cannot be condoned. Northern Ireland is an operational theatre and this is a very serious matter.

"The men are now anxiously awaiting the results of the second test. If these tests prove positive as well, the consequences could be dire.

"But nothing has yet been proved conclusively." The Army's Special Investigation Branch acted after a "report" was secretly handed to top

brass at the base in Ballykelly, near Londonderry.

It listed the names of men allegedly spotted at the nightclub on Thursday and Saturday of last week. Senior officers were told the soldiers had been taking Ecstasy which has side effects that can kill.

The near 600-strong battalion has been in Ulster for six months and is on a two-year tour of duty.

An Army spokesman last night confirmed an inquiry had been launched.

He added: "We cannot anticipate the outcome yet."

Motto: Death Before Dishonour

nity to unburden themselves, and many wrote of their own experiences which added to the original information.

Former soldiers told how the 'yellow card' instructions about the circumstances in which soldiers could open fire were abused. To detain an Arab, soldiers were taught to shout 'waqaf' – pronounced 'wakeef' – meaning 'halt'. If three warnings were ignored, soldiers were entitled to shoot, but some treated this as a joke and shouted 'corned beef' instead. Not surprisingly, most Arabs did not understand this and several were gunned down.

The army had machine-gun emplacements overlooking the Crater district. Each night, if there had been conflict involving soldiers, those heavy guns were fired into the shanty-town as a punishment. The heavy bullets ripped through the thin walls of the poor people's dwellings, causing untold death and destruction.

If these revelations had been the result of the actions of a small section of overzealous soldiers, it would have been bad enough. But a further – and the most horrific – revelation concerned the inter-platoon rivalry initiated by officers, who awarded Robertson's jam golliwog stickers to units for each killing of an Arab. An ex-soldier wrote:

> At one stage my platoon had notched up thirteen kills and another
> platoon were one kill behind. Their corporal even told the privates to use
> their bayonets, for it was to be that sort of killing. They went into an alley and
> killed a young Arab who was out after curfew.[48]

Aden was following the same pattern as Malaya and Kenya, where army units had kept 'kills' scoreboards too.

The *Sunday Mail* passed the dossier to the Scottish Lord Advocate who promised an investigation. But this time there was no pressing reason to examine these events. Two years later the *Sunday Mail* printed a tiny article saying the Lord Advocate had decided no proceedings should be instituted. The military unit involved in those incidents in County Fermanagh and Aden was the Argyll and Sutherland Highlanders, a regiment with an official history as proud and honourable as any in the British Army. They were led in Aden by the British 'hero' Lieutenant-Colonel Colin 'Mad Mitch' Mitchell, who later left the army and became a Tory MP.

In 1970, as British soldiers were asserting their presence across nationalist areas in Northern Ireland, Russel Stetler wrote a prophetic article for the American magazine *Monthly Review*:

> More than any country in the West, Britain has fostered the myth of a non-violent, civilised society, symbolised by the unarmed London bobby. …
> Even in its period of greatest peace at home, Britain was fighting a series of Vietnams throughout its former colonies (Malaya, Kenya and Aden). Today
> …Vietnam has come home to Britain, in the armed resistance of the colonised Irish within a territory which the British claim as part of the United Kingdom.[49]

As with Vietnam, the reality of the series of small wars fought by the British army after 1945 was hidden behind a curtain of chauvinism, misrepresentations and propaganda. Most of the population in Britain did not want to know anyway, and turned a blind eye, leaving the soldiers, recruited from the most marginalised sectors of society and controlled and directed by the officer-class ideologues of counterrevolutionary warfare, to fight those colonial wars in isolation.

Subsequently, many soldiers who fought in Britain's colonial wars have dark secrets which were kept bottled up in young minds. These have been revealed only in exceptional circumstances, as when that Scottish ex-soldier in his mid-twenties entered a Glasgow police station in 1978 telling the startled police about the 'pitchfork murders', 'which had been on his conscience for six years'.

The Falklands and the Gulf

In spring 1982 a British invasion fleet set sail for the Falklands. IRN radio reporter Kim Sabido travelled with the troops. Some reporters had complained about the strict censorship enforced by minders, but its existence was always denied by the government. When Sabido returned to Britain, he told Duncan Campbell of the London listings magazine *City Limits* of his experiences: 'We were told that the only censorship would be about our military plans and our position. But this turned out to be completely untrue, the tone of pieces was constantly censored.' Sabido continued:

When the marines spat at the black people bringing things on board in Freetown we were told we couldn't report that.

... There was a lot about how young the Argentinian soldiers were, but when we tried to report on the ages of our marines – the average age was 19 and there were some 17-year-olds that NCOs thought were too young – we were told it wasn't a story. We thought they had to be 18 to go into combat, but we were told this wasn't the case, and therefore it wasn't worth our while to do a story.

And when I filed a story about how shocked people were after the sinking of the Sheffield, I was told by one of the minders – the most despicable of men – that there was no shock. I was typing the story out in the bar and he came up and told me that I couldn't say people were shocked.

When we landed and 20 people were killed I reported that it had been a much bloodier day than was expected and I was told that I would have to take that out if I wanted to get it through – so all the time the tone was being censored.

... Most of the marines and paras would say that it had all been worth it, but a lot of the troops were unhappy. ... Prince Andrew said that after what he'd seen he felt like joining the Campaign for Nuclear Disarmament, but that was after the tape had been turned off.[50]

Some of the fighting could have been avoided. But back in Britain, whipped up by the media and politicians, the mood was distinctly jingoistic and the government wanted victories. Sabido told about the battle for Goose Green:

The Battle of Goose Green – where 17 paras and about 120 Argentinians died – was a politician's battle not a soldier's one: we were told both before and after that there was no need to attack, Goose Green could have been isolated. But Brigadier Julian Thompson had been called to the satellite phone to talk to a politician – we were told it was Mrs Thatcher but this was not confirmed – and after that the whole emphasis changed and an attack was launched.

... When some of the soldiers had been under fire for two hours and were in among the Argentinian positions, they became hysterical, it was almost like a sexual experience for some of them. They were shouting 'where are the bastards? Give me a grenade' and their officers had to physically restrain them. They also shot two people in the back who had thrown down their weapons. Two paras also looted the vet's house of £2000 worth of silver.[51]

As in many previous conflicts, the sanitised views of the Falklands war received at home were contradicted by the actual happening on the battlefields. In the bitter fighting on Mount Longdon, twenty-three soldiers from 3 Para were killed and thirty-five were wounded. Afterwards, there were allegations of atrocities which journalists from TV's *World in Action* investigated: 'On our programme, the father of a corporal killed on Longdon said he believed his son had been denied a battle honour because the battalion padre had found severed ears, apparently collected as war trophies, in his kit. We established from Para officers that this was true.' *World in Action* continued:

> What about the worst claims – those of killing unarmed prisoners of war? For the first time, we told how a former lance-corporal had made a tape-recording, describing how he and a colleague had machine-gunned three POWs they believed to be American mercenaries, during the battle.

> Most compelling of all was the appearance of Tony Mason, at the time of the battle a captain, later a major, in 3 Para. Calmly, and with assurance, he described witnessing the killing of a prisoner, the morning after the battle, by a body-pit on Mt Longdon. 'I heard somebody shouting.' he said. 'I saw a young soldier being dragged to the edge of what was essentially an open grave. [He] was shot over the grave. He was shot in the head. That is what I saw.'[52]

A lot of the death and destruction was delivered from a distance, by aircraft and heavy guns. But, much of the fighting was reminiscent of the First World War. Many of the soldiers like Scots Guardsman Frank Gilchrist became involved in hand-to-hand combat:

> Once you get in close, say about 30 feet away, you engage in what is called fight-through. When you have fought your way through the first and second trenches you find yourself in the centre with loads of men running about, so it is quite easy to shoot your own.

The best thing to do then is to use your bayonet. This was happening a lot at Tumbledown and frankly, in that sort of situation you sort of go mad – maybe it's the adrenalin ...

When you are actually fighting you can feel and smell the deaths. If you stab someone with a bayonet you feel the blood run down your hands, you feel them kicking. Afterwards you could see people being sick ... [53]

As the British Task Force had sped towards the South Atlantic many of the soldiers had sailed in cruise liners, converted to carry the troops. In the evenings the soldiers were often entertained by the regimental bands playing a selection of popular tunes. A favourite was the old Cliff Richard hit 'Summer Holiday', to which the soldiers sang along, adding their own words. At Westminster, the political parties competed to show who was the most patriotic. As the politicians spoke in impassioned terms, drumming up popular support for the coming war, the soldiers on the ships voiced their intentions in song:

We're all going on a summer holiday,

We're all gonna kill a spic or two

Three months later 1,800 Argentinian servicemen were dead, missing or wounded. 256 British soldiers and sailors were killed and 777 wounded. There were also the hidden casualties, those left with post-traumatic stress disorders. Frank Gilchrist later left the army and turned to drugs to blot out his memory of the fighting. He contracted AIDS through sharing syringes while injecting heroin. Gilchrist later said about the fighting, 'When we were going through the trenches and seeing lots of corpses, like someone who has been shot through the mouth, I can always remember thinking that the politicians who sent us should come and bury the dead.' [54]

Alex Findlay, a corporal in the Scots Guards, also fought on Mount Tumbledown. One of his friends was badly injured during the fighting:

He was gurgling on his own blood and he couldn't speak. Something was wrong with his breathing. I tried clearing his airways, but clots of blood were coming out. He was asking me to shoot him and trying to shoot himself with his own rifle. That's how much pain the guy was in. Then he just stopped breathing on me. What do you do? Just run away and leave the guy, or try and do something?[55]

Findlay stayed and carried out a tracheotomy, using his bayonet to stab into his mate's throat and create a new airway. His friend survived, but later Findlay himself was badly wounded in a mortar attack. Back home, after the war, he turned to drink. Findlay's wife suffered years of violent abuse; finally having had an ear-drum burst by one of his blows, she threw him out. She stated, 'Alex had changed when he came back from the Falklands. He had a lot of nightmares, where he used to sweat like a pig. But he kept it all inside because it was too traumatic an experience. They offered them no help at all. So there was a lot of drinking.'[56]

Findlay's regiment was then posted on a tour of duty in Northern Ireland. He told his officers he was suffering from stress and pleaded not to be sent. He was ordered to go, but cracked when a colleague opened a beer can and the noise reminded him of a bullet whizzing past his ear:

> ... one night in Northern Ireland, in July 1990, the snap of a beer can opening finally unhinged Alex. Brandishing a pistol, he threatened to shoot the other members of his company, then himself. An Army psychiatrist told him he was suffering from PTSD, but the prosecution at his courtmartial rejected the idea and he was sentenced to two years in prison.[57]

After his release from prison and the army, Findlay was determined to prove that he had been unjustly treated by the military authorities. So he hired a lawyer and set out to sue the MoD for failing to diagnose or treat his PTSD. Just before the case was due to be heard, Findlay accepted £100,000 from the MoD in an out-of-court settlement; 'The Defence Ministry settled without accepting liability, Mr Findlay's solicitor said.'[58] Findlay then took his case to the European Court of Human Rights. It ruled that he had been dealt with unfairly because his court martial had failed to take into account his medical condition:

> Falklands veteran Alex Findlay has thrown the future of Army court martials into doubt after winning a historic legal battle.
>
> The ex-Scots Guard spent two years in jail after going berserk at a barracks in Ulster.
>
> ... The judgement could land Army bosses with a multi-million pound

compensation bill from other service personnel who believe they too were treated unfairly.'[59]

Towards the end of 1982 the *Guardian* journalist Polly Toynbee, interviewed Surgeon Commander Morgan O'Connell who had just returned from the Falklands where he had treated battle-shocked soldiers and sailors. O'Connell's role as a psychiatrist was not welcomed by everyone – to the extent that when he was on board a ship and summoned by tannoy, a pseudonym was often used; 'If the men heard my name called all sorts of stories would go round. They'd say "Someone's thrown a wobbly again", or "Who's slashed their wrists this time?"' Toynbee described how the interview 'was only permitted in the presence of a "minder"':

> I asked Cdr. O'Connell how many men he, and his psychiatric colleague ... had treated. The minder stepped in here briskly to say that 32 men of the task force were still under psychiatric treatment. But how many, I asked, had been treated in the first place?
>
> On October 18 Alf Morris asked a parliamentary question about the exact numbers of wounded, and the nature of their wounds. In the list he elicited from Defence Minister Peter Baker only 17 men are reported as "shock" cases yet 32 are now officially being treated. Cdr. O'Connell asserted vigorously when he heard the figures, "I treated well over a 100 myself"...
>
> The minder telephoned me the same day as soon as I was back in my office to say he hoped there weren't any misunderstandings. ... The trouble with psychiatric illness, he said, was that you couldn't see it. Presumably that is why such cases are less visible that they might be in the official figures.[60]

In 1991, Gary Roberts was sent to the Gulf with his unit, the 1st Battalion of the Staffordshire Regiment. He was there for six months and took part in the conflict, helping to overrun Iraqi trenches. Roberts received a leg wound in a 'friendly fire' incident, but soldiered on till the fighting stopped. Afterwards, he required three operations for his wounds, and then was granted leave. Back home his mother, Maureen, commented:

> 'It was clear immediately that something was terribly wrong. He drank

masses. All he did was get up, go out, drink and shout'.

'Half-way through his seven-week leave, he broke down watching television pictures of the Kurdish refugees in northern Iraq. ... He kept saying: "We've done that, it's our fault." Then his eyes glazed over and he started to strangle me. I lay on the floor because I couldn't fight my own son and he was too strong; he just got up and ran out.'

After a night sleeping rough, Gary returned home and poured out his heart to his parents. 'He was sobbing. He said, "I need help, mum, I need help." He told my husband what he had done, that he'd gone into the Iraqi trenches and found men with no feet, and others dead, the same age as his sister, who was then 13. And an old man dead, clutching a shopping bag with his possessions.'

Mrs Roberts rang an army careers office and asked for advice. 'They simply told me, tell us who it is and we'll come and get the little bastard. He needs to be locked up.'[61]

Back with his unit in Germany, Gary and a number of other soldiers were travelling in two cars which were stopped and searched by the military police, and a quantity of cannabis was found. In order to help her son, Maureen Roberts contacted his unit, but she was reassured by those in charge; 'Officers and other soldiers told Mrs Roberts that Gary and the others had "nothing to worry about". The regiment, she was told, was awash with cannabis after the Gulf war.'[62]

In light of this, Gary and four other soldiers pleaded guilty at their court martial, which was held in Northern Ireland. However, the soldiers' Gulf war experiences were not accepted as mitigation and they were sentenced to seven months' imprisonment, then dismissal from service. In the draconian environment of an army prison, Gary's condition deteriorated:

The prison psychiatrist at Colchester has prescribed daily doses of tranquillisers and anti-depressant drugs. His mother, Maureen Roberts, ... described a visit to her son ... : 'He was smiling but his eyes were dead. It was as if he was there but not there at the same time.'

... Mrs Roberts said: 'They tell me that, on the day of Gary's release, they will give him his breakfast and his medication and discharge him, and leave it up to me to seek further help. When it came to the crunch and he had to serve his country he was not found wanting. Now the army couldn't care less.'[63]

Vietnam Syndrome

Many of the soldiers who fought in the Falklands and the Gulf were Northern Ireland veterans. Most returned to tours of duty in Belfast, Derry or the border areas. Years earlier, on 25th February 1979, Trooper Edward Maggs was shot dead in west Belfast. At the time, his death was front page news, different from the usual couple of sentences, '... another soldier killed ...', printed at the bottom of page 5. According to military sources, Maggs had been drinking inside the Woodburn Army base when he had suddenly started firing at other soldiers, killing Corporal John Tucker and seriously injuring Lance Corporal David Mellor, before he himself was shot dead by fellow soldiers. His father, retired bank official Douglas Maggs, said:

We don't know what went wrong yet. All we've been told is that Eddie cracked up, ran amok with a rifle and was shot dead by another soldier to prevent further bloodshed.

This wouldn't have happened if he hadn't been sent to Northern Ireland for a second time.

He was a victim of Northern Ireland just as surely as if he'd been shot in the back by a sniper's bullet.

My son loved the Army, but four months out there last year finished him. He was terrified of going back.

He planned to get out before his 21st birthday this September, and he'd applied for a job as a fireman in London.

He was a good soldier, and I only hope that some good will come out of this tragedy.[64]

His mother, Pamela Maggs, added, 'We adopted Eddie when he was six. Before he came to us his life had been rotten. We gave him all the love we could. He was always crazy about being a soldier, but he was desperately scared of returning to Northern Ireland.'[65]

It was evident, even from the early days, that many squaddies were fed up with their role in Northern Ireland. In April 1974, Christopher Dobson – 'With the troops in Ulster's ugly world of terrorism' – filed this report in the *Sunday Telegraph*: 'To walk along Belfast's Royal Avenue today is like walking in the past – along Ledra Street in Nicosia when Eoka's murderers were at work. Venturing into the Bogside in Derry is like taking a patrol into Aden's Crater district, and dropping by helicopter into a border fort is like visiting a fire-base in Vietnam.' Under the heading 'ANGER OF ARMY THAT FEELS BETRAYED' Dobson continued:

> So far more than 200 British soldiers have been killed while many more have been maimed. The soldiers' work is hard, their pay is low and more often than not they receive curses instead of thanks from the people for whom they are dying.
>
> There can be no surprise therefore that the average soldier is thoroughly fed up with Ireland and everything to do with it. But what surprised me was the extent and depth of the bitterness that exists among the troops, some of whom are on their fifth tour of duty in Ulster.
>
> I met a section who had just returned from an 'Eagle patrol' – lifted in by helicopter to set a snap road block. They were tired, dirty and remarkably frank. I said to them: 'Tell me what it is all about.' Their officers were present and I believe that they were also surprised at the depth of feeling that the troops displayed.
>
> Soldiers are expected to grumble, but these men genuinely felt that they were being misused and ill-treated. Their complaints ranged over pay, excessively long hours, of being "forgotten", and in particular the inability of "the bloody politicians" to settle the appalling mess in which the soldiers found themselves targets of both sides.[66]

August 1979, seven months after Eddie Maggs was shot dead in west Belfast, saw the tenth anniversary of the war in Northern Ireland. *Time Out*, a London listings magazine, detailed some statistics of the conflict. On its front page, under a headline which read 'TEN YEARS OF TROOPS IN IRELAND. THE FAILURE OF BRITISH PEACEKEEPING' *Time Out* listed:

- [ ] 1932 Dead.
- [ ] 20421 Injured.
- [ ] 26516 Shootings.
- [ ] 6309 Explosions.
- [ ] 3018 Bombs neutralised.
- [ ] 8076 Armed robberies.
- [ ] 2736 Malicious fires.
- [ ] £276,000,000 Damages compensation.
- [ ] £46,000,000 Injury compensation.[67]

In 1994, the writer Timothy O'Grady interviewed victims from all sides of the conflict. One was a ex-soldier who had served a tour of duty in Northern Ireland with the Royal Anglian Regiment. He had joined the army at seventeen; 'I'd been farming since I left school. Then I was given a year's notice. There was nothing else around. I'd seen the ads for the Army, all about the glory and the travel around the world. I thought, "Sod it," and I went to the recruitment office in Leicester and signed up.' In Northern Ireland he was billeted at the North Howard Street barracks in west Belfast; 'I had this idea about the place. I thought there'd be these cartoon-like people running around with guns and bombs with lit fuses. But most of the time it's just like here. ... Sometimes you'd be fired at. You'd be in a place like Beechmount and hear something twanging off the wall behind you. Maybe you'd beat a few Irish people up. Then you'd go back. The kids are the main problem. They'd put their dogs on you. They'd throw paint bombs, petrol bombs, tellies, dirty nappies at you. It was nerve-wracking, but it was real.' The veteran then told O'Grady about his last patrol:

We were going from Springfield Road RUC station to North Howard Street. I was the last man in the patrol. We were 400 metres from the camp, walking with a factory wall to one side and a building site to the other. It was enclosed in corrugated iron.

I saw a flash. You always see a flash before you hear the explosion. I put my hands up to my ears. That is what saved me from being killed, the hands protecting my head from the shrapnel. It was a beer barrel packed with explosives, a CWIED as we call them – a Command Wire Ignited Electronic

Device. It had been detonated from a pub.

When my girlfriend came to see me I was listed as clinically dead. My right leg was off above the knee where a piece of the barrel had hit it. I lost the left leg below the knee when gangrene set in. I lost my right eye. There was shrapnel just two millimetres from my brain. They put 20 pints of blood into me but my body rejected it. Maybe if it had been 20 pints of bitter I'd have been all right.

When I started to come around my girlfriend gave me full-wack stick. She wasn't going to let me feel sorry for myself. She pushed me to get up on my legs and learn to walk again. We got married when I was going through rehabilitation in London. They told me I could never have kids, but they were wrong. We have two, a boy and a girl.

I get angry much easier now. If I can't work the lawn mower I might just throw it as far as I can. The worst part of it is not being able to be a normal father to my kids.

As for the Army and what they do for you, do you want a joke? The first year's all right, then they forget about you. When the regiment asked me if there was anything I wanted I said a video. They sent it over with the rental papers. They sent me my Northern Ireland service medal in a Jiffy bag.[68]

For nearly three decades, British soldiers in Ireland have been shot dead, blown to bits by bombs and endured taunts and missiles from hostile crowds. Many soldiers who would have died in more conventional conflicts were saved – only because they could be rushed to expert medical treatment. Some live out their lives with terrible wounds, from which they will never recover. Certain soldiers performed heroic acts, providing protection from sectarian violence or rescuing people from bombings or other life-threatening situations. Life for soldiers in Ireland usually amounted to long periods of isolation and boredom, punctuated by brief, often intense, episodes of violence and mayhem. IRA actions in Britain left soldiers feeling on edge and vulnerable even after coming home. Many veterans found they could not leave the war behind; 'When I went back on leave, the first day I went out shopping with my sister we were walking down the street and a car came past and backfired. Before I knew what I was doing I'd

The magazine that tells you what's on and where to go in London.
August 10-16 1979 No.486 35p

Time Out

TEN YEARS OF TROOPS IN IRELAND. THE FAILURE OF BRITISH PEACE KEEPING.

1932 Dead.
20421 Injured.
26516 Shootings.
6309 Explosions.
3018 Bombs neutralised.
8076 Armed robberies.
2736 Malicious fires.
£276,000,000 Damage compensation.
£46,000,000 Injury compensation.

Angry ex-Para pushed 'suicide' girl off bridge

By David Graves

A FORMER Colour Sergeant in the Parachute Regiment who had served in the Falklands was jailed for 15 months yesterday for pushing a woman, who was threatening to jump from a railway bridge, on to the tracks because she was delaying his train.

Police had been patiently trying ... er down when lea... ... went to the bri... station ... delays ...

Naked soldier denies assault

A PARATROOPER from Cheriton celebrated his discharge with a full frontal strip act in a pub in front of five Army nurses, a court heard.

The nurses, all 21, and students at Aldershot Cambridge Military Hospital, ... slapped the ... nurses, and of causing actual bodily harm to one of them.

In the dock with him are serving paratroopers Andrew Cook, 22, who denies causing actual bodily harm to the same nurse Jennifer Burridge, Martin Jones, 20, Ricky Hopkins, 24, and Ian Bissett, 26, who with Rellis and Cook plead not guilty to causing a...

Nurse ... told the cou...

near me."

She said the man then grabbed nurse Burridge from behind. She slapped him across the face. Someone behind the naked man grabbed her hair, pulled her down, kneed her in the face and then others joined in. They jumped on top of her, hit and ... ...ingway tried ... ... from under ...

Soldier guilty of indecent assault

A SOLDIER has been found guilty of indecently assaulting a colleague's three-year-old daughter at the CAD army base at Kineton, Warwickshire.

... (26), of CAD ... denied ... ...ting the girl in ... at the base last

... more than 3½ ... jury at Warwick ... court found him guilty. ... Paul Clark adjourned ... for reports and Aller... ... ...manded in custody.

...ayed

... heard that ... ...ack to the ... ...arents for ... ...ence on the ... ... night. ... ...morning he played ... ... and her young ... ... then offered to ... ...reed. ... ...utes later her ...ted to her ... ...uard. my ... ...door and ... ...r sitting on a ... ...clothes on.

...rrested

...dice left she and ...poke to the girl ...the police who

Falklands hero sen... to prison

THE law's sympathy for ... ex-paratrooper severely ... burned in the Falklands War finally ran out yesterday.

At Warwick Crown Court ... Judge Michael Harrison Hall jailed Mark Richard for nine months for breach of probation.

Richard, of Solihull, West Midlands, had twice earlier this year been given chances and put on probation. The first was for theft, the second for attacking his love ... with a poker.

But he visited a prob... attendance centre only ... times out of 25.

Liverpool Daily ... 15.12...

SHOCK SUICIDE OF THE FIVE TROOPS WHO CRACKED

FIVE soldiers have cracked up and killed themselves while serving in Northern Ireland in the last two years.

Fifteen more have been flown home following checks by psychiatrists.

These disclosures by the Army last night follow the tragedy of Trooper Edward Maggs, shot dead by a marksman on Sunday after he ran amok with a rifle.

Maggs, 26, began shooting inside the Woodburn base in West Belfast. When two NCOs tried to persuade him to surrender, he killed one and seriously wounded the other.

All the deaths from stress happened despite a continual vetting of the mental state of soldiers.

The Ministry of Defence said "There is no psychiatrist stationed in Northern Ireland, but a visiting psychiatrist flies in once a fortnight. ...

"On average, he sees three soldiers a month."

Medical officers are on constant alert for signs of a nervous breakdown. "Anyone showing serious symptoms is sent home at once," said an Army

MAGGS: Shot when he ran amok

By DOUGLAS BENCE

With more than 13,000 troops serving in Northern Ireland, the number is ...

Maggs before he was shot — and the soldier who pulled the trigger. Trooper Maggs's father, Douglas Maggs, 56, said at his home in Walton-on-the-Naze, Essex, last ...

Boy, 4, 'terribly burned' by soldier's home-made bomb

The Sun 20 Sep 88

A FOUR-YEAR-OLD boy's life was "totally ruined" when he was turned into a human fireball by a soldier's home-made bomb, the Old Bailey was told yesterday.

The bomb, made with stolen Army materials by James Cobb, 19, of the Royal Green Jackets, exploded in Michael Walsh's hand when he found it near his home in Putney, south-west London.

The boy was covered in a scorching, sticky substance which burnt away the skin on his head and chest, and it was "miraculous" that his life had been saved.

A consultant plastic surgeon said: "Michael sustained terrible burns. He is left with permanent mutilating scarring and will need a great deal of reconstructive surgery. He will have very unusual and noticeable facial markings and will need to wear pressure garments for another year or two.

"After that he will need a protracted series of reconstructive ...

JUDGE AIDS ARMY 'PAL'

The Sun 17 May 91

A WAR hero judge dramatically intervened in a trial yesterday to save an ex-soldier from his regiment.

Phillip Routledge—an ex-lance corporal with the Queen's Regiment—went berserk and barricaded himself in his home with a mini-arsenal of weapons. He felt "every street" had treated him badly.

But Old Bailey judge Michael Argyle QC told 38-year-old Routledge: "You are very lucky to come in front of me.

"In 1944 I led your regiment across the river." ... "You can make ... ...ha... ...volve ... ...of th... ...T... ...that ... ...You ... ...that, ...body's ... ...ger an... ...Mr... ...oute... ...has...

Judge Argyle interrupted defence counsel summing up to reveal that he had already conducted the regiment, confident.

He told Routledge, of Carshalton, Surrey: "The regiment is standing by you. Try to get a job."

...ie milk bottle with ... ...urged th... ...which stick to their target and how to make improvised bombs, was inscribed: "To James Cobb with best wishes. I hope you have lots of fun at home and that you still have a home at the end of it."

American publication which ap-...ters devoted to jellied flame fuels ...

Mr Cobb allegedly told police ...

Police investigate deaths at farm

The deaths of Mr Peter Miller, aged about 35, a farmer, and Rifleman Christopher Radmore, aged 23, of the 1st Battalion, The Royal Green Jackets, at Great Farchingdon Farm, Dover, where a fire occurred yesterday, are being investigated last night by detectives.

Police officers were called to the farm when firemen found Mr Miller dead upstairs. Later a man with two children, was found dead in the basement near piles of charred wood. The farm was not badly damaged.

He shot dead his wife and baby, now 14 months later he's back up the aisle

Sun EXCLUSIVE

By PATRICK GRIFFIN

FREED killer Graham Sherman, who blasted his wife and baby to death with a shotgun, married his teenage girlfriend yesterday.

And bride Cheryl, who expects his baby in two weeks, said: "I can never think of Graham as a killer.— he is my husband and I love him very much."

A storm erupted when ex-Royal Marine Sherman, 22, was freed after being convicted of the manslaughter of Michelle, 23, and one-month-old Joan.

Controversial Judge Dunpark said he was a "devoted" husband and dad who had already punished himself enough. The judge said no one could ...

jumped over a garden wall and was crouching down behind it. My sister burst into tears. She said it was horrible to see me like that.'[69]

American soldiers who became alienated from the war in Vietnam, or who developed sympathetic feelings towards the Vietnamese people, suffered disproportionally afterwards:

> Blacks, vet-for-vet, have many more cases of PTSD than vets in general. According to Legacies of Vietnam, a 1981 study commissioned by Congress ... nearly 70 per cent of blacks who were in heavy combat suffer some degree of PTSD. The figure for whites is 'only' 23 per cent. The percentage may be so much higher for blacks partly because blacks as a group were more sympathetic than whites towards the Vietnamese people and were more opposed to the war. As a result, they presumably suffered more guilt in connection with the killings and brutalisation of Vietnamese soldiers and civilians.[70]

Irish soldiers in the British army, like former Royal Marine Derek McAdam, often felt a conflict of loyalties when the strife in Northern Ireland started. McAdam was discharged from the army suffering from depression:

> ... it has taken almost 20 years to prove that action in Northern Ireland has mentally affected the Dublin-born Royal Marine. Now, at last, 60-year-old Derek has been awarded a lump sum of £25,000 and a pension of almost £200 a week.
>
> ... it was in the early 1970s when he was posted to Northern Ireland that things started to go wrong. Derek said: 'I was a weapons instructor and I was training commandos to shoot my countrymen. This split in loyalties began to make me very depressed and I was sent to a military psychiatric hospital.'
>
> He was discharged but the MoD and DHSS refused to accept his depression had been caused by his service in Ireland. [71]

In Northern Ireland, many soldiers became frustrated and suffered from alienation. Some took it out on the 'enemy', which often meant any nationalists they came in contact with. Others just cracked up; some soldiers brought these problems home. In 1992, the *Irish Post*, the paper of the Irish community in Britain, reported the fate of such a veteran: 'A British soldier's Northern Ireland experiences led him to commit suicide, a Lancashire inquest into his death has decided.' *The Irish Post* continued:

> Stanley Farrell, a 24-year-old from Bootle, Merseyside, ... was found dead in his fume-filled car last month.
>
> Philip Farrell told Coroner Howard McCann that his son joined the British Army aged 18 and left in December 1990.
>
> His son felt Northern Ireland's problems 'could have been resolved quite easily' but the father revealed last week that Stanley Farrell developed personal difficulties of his own through what he saw on Irish streets.[72]

Comparisons of conventional wars with other conflicts – say the Normandy landings with Vietnam or Northern Ireland – shows that the scale and intensity of fighting is undoubtedly greater in the former. But, other factors made soldiers serving tours of duty in Northern Ireland or Vietnam particularly prone to psychiatric disorders, especially after leaving the services. Many aspects of military operations and the subsequent actions of the soldiers were hidden from the home populations. Like the GIs in Vietnam, British soldiers occupying nationalist areas in Northern Ireland often had difficulty in even deciding who the enemy was: 'Standard rubrics of traditional warfare, as for example "the only good German is a dead German", cannot be trusted in a conflict in which a dead Irishman may well turn out to have been a good Irishman. The basic distinction between good and bad – ours and theirs – is missing in a conflict when they cannot be reliably separated from another larger group – the innocent.'[73] Back home, like many Vietnam veterans, some British soldiers who had served in Northern Ireland began to have doubts about their role in the conflict:

> During my first tour I remember remarking to a corporal, 'If I'd been born here, I think I could have joined the IRA.'
>
> Not because I respected them, but because I could see what it was like for the poor people in the ghetto areas. It was different from Bradford where we had kicked a ball around in the streets. Here there was no peace. I could see how they looked at it, being harassed by soldiers from overseas who could wreck their houses and laugh at them from behind our guns. I could even understand why some of them used violence in return.

But at that time I made the simple point that it was my duty to put down violence. I thought I was right because I was backed by the Government, the Law and the majority of the British People.

Later I changed my mind. They call the IRA terrorists, but the longer I thought about it, the more I began to wonder who the real terrorists were. For a guy drinking his pint and watching the telly it's simple who the baddies are, but such a person does not know the history of the situation or about the oppression or harassment.[74]

Conventional wars are generally supported by the home population. Battles are fought, in the main, according to certain rules, and returning soldiers are heroes who can talk about their experiences to an admiring and supportive audience. Conflicts like Vietnam or Northern Ireland, on the other hand, are usually secretive and dirty affairs, with much of the violence clandestine and brutal. Like GIs returning from Vietnam, British soldiers going home from Ireland often faced an unresponsive or sometimes hostile population – who generally did not want or were even unwilling to listen to tales about the conflict:

I had the impression that they did not understand or did not want to hear. The army is a world apart on its own, but Northern Ireland is like another planet. Back home they only relate to the 9 o'clock news, but that is far from the reality of the situation. Even to my wife, I told her very little about the army and Northern Ireland. Nobody knows that I'm still looking for snipers. I'm not afraid of being killed, but walking down a street or driving on a motorway I keep noticing; this spot could be an ambush. It's a reflex, I left the army and Northern Ireland, but the army and Northern Ireland is still within me.[75]

Relatives of soldiers killed or injured while serving tours of duty were often upset by the insensitive treatment dished out by the authorities. In 1990, the *Daily Mail* told how 'The mother of an IRA victim has attacked the Government after getting half the compensation paid out to a farmer who lost an animal.' The *Daily Mail* continued:

Mrs Irene Macaulay's 20-year-old paratrooper son Donald was one of three soldiers killed by a booby trap bomb in Northern Ireland two months ago.

She received £2,250 compensation from the Government – and has complained that a farmer in Cumbria was paid £5,000 when his Llama was killed during RAF manoeuvres.

... She also claimed that one of the soldiers who was badly injured in the same attack, Lee Manning, has been told his overseas pay will be stopped if he does not start patrolling the streets again within 21 days.[76]

The first soldier fatalities in Northern Ireland featured prominently on the front pages of British papers. At the end of 1972 the magazine *New Society* did a survey of 100 British soldiers killed in Northern Ireland between January and November of that year:

77 were privates, of whom 47 were twenty-two years or under when killed. Only six came from the seven largest cities of Britain, whilst most were from market towns in the West Country, the Fens, or small industrial centres in Lancashire, Tyneside, Scotland or Wales. On average it was the less educated boy who has to leave home to have a hope of employment who joins the British Army.[77]

Partly due to these deaths, Westminster politicians knew that among the British people there was widespread disillusionment with the ongoing conflict. Ireland, therefore, had to become a forgotten war. Prominent details of soldiers' deaths in papers would have prevented this, so subsequent reports moved gradually from the headlines to a few sentences on an inside page. Refusing to allow the names of soldiers killed in Northern Ireland to be added to war memorials was another issue that caused distress to soldiers and their relatives. As *Soldier* magazine reported:

It is saddening that unseemly wrangling over the commemoration of soldiers killed in Northern Ireland has followed in the wake of the Warrenpoint Massacre in which nearly a score of soldiers were slaughtered.

Press reports have told of the powers-that-be in towns and villages where some of the dead came from, refusing to allow the soldiers' names to be added to the local war memorials.

... All manner of shuffle-footed justification have been offered as excuses

Death of a soldier

Soldier who 'cracked' to be returned

By our Correspondents

The soldier absent without leave from his post in Ulster who was arrested by police in Northamptonshire on Saturday is expected to be handed into military custody today.

Corporal Roger Schofield, aged 30, of the 3rd Battalion Royal Greenjackets, failed to report for duty in Derry on Friday night. He apparently crossed unrecognised by ferry to Britain and drove to Northamptonshire where, when arrested, he was still armed with a 9mm army pistol and 14 rounds of ammunition.

No shots were fired during the three hours when armed police surrounded the house in Earl's Barton where he had hidden.

"We understand the police are not preferring charges, but are holding Corporal Schofield until tomorrow," said an army spokesman in Northern Ireland last night. "He will then be handed over into military custody and taken to the Green-jackets depot at Winchester. It is not known when, if at all, he will be returned here."

Mrs Pauline Pickering, divorced mother of four, wants to marry him, said yesterday: "He cracked under the pressure of the war in Ireland."

But she added: "I love him and will be standing by him."

Police were alerted after Cpl Schofield, a married man, had left his unit at Ebrington Barracks, Londonderry. He has been stationed in Ulster for 13 months.

He and his girl friend arrived at the home of a mutual friend, Mrs Sandra Dickson, on Saturday morning. More than 20 police, many including a special unit set up to deal with sieges, handled the affair. They surrounded the house.

Also in the house were Mrs Dickson and two of her children, Cindy, 19 and Richard, aged eight, pounced after the siege and the children had left.

Superintendent Ken and Detective-Inspector Sharp, armed and let-proof vests, burst house through the Corporal Schofield on the settee with sion switched on.

Mrs Dickson police

Soldier held

A soldier serving in Belfast, who may have been trying to secure his discharge from the Army, was yesterday fired nine shots at the door of a building, housing the American consulate here. He made sure no one was by the door before firing. He was questioned before being taken into custody.

DAILY TIMES

Crazed Ulster veteran in gun siege terror

Court told how ex-soldier relived ordeal in village

HOME N

12/4/79 Guardian

Brain-damaged soldiers 'serving in Ulster'

By Peter Chippindale

SOLDIERS still suffering serious brain damage are put back on active duty in Northern Ireland when they come out of hospital, it is claimed today.

The allegation is to be made tonight in a Thames Television documentary by a Army doctor who treats a consultant surgeon who treated men for three years until it was...

Dr Hugh Thomas, consultant to the Royal Charles Hospital, Merthyr St. South Wales. He treated soldiers who were in for treatment for injuries, pressure put on them by units and doctors to return to duty before they had fully covered. Soldiers who he downgraded, or who thought would take con-valesce were going on duty.

When asked why, he was still in the army Thomas says: "He salute and stand up and put are two very important requisites for army service. He ought to have been picked up long ago ... He was called dumb by his colleagues. They were calling him clumsy. He became the butt of the unit and they ought to have put thim on from that point of view."

Dr Thomas says that a number of occasions he tried to do something about the men but could not...

Crown inquiry on IRA 'sympathiser' serving 9 years

The Crown is investigating the case of a young Scots Guardsman, John Boyle, jailed for nine years for armed bank robbery.

His counsel, Mr. Donald Robertson, Q.C., told the Court of Criminal Appeal on Friday in Edinburgh that there was serious doubt as to whether Boyle was involved in the crime—to which he pleaded guilty. Boyle (21) was jailed in November. He was said to be an I.R.A. sympathiser, but not a member. He admitted robbing the Royal Bank in Argyll Street, Glasgow.

The court heard he was persuaded to rob the bank to get funds for the I.R.A. by a man called Pat, who gave him £200 for the hold-up.

On Friday, Boyle was to have appealed against the length of his sentence, but Mr. Robertson asked for an investigation of the whole case instead.

The Solicitor-General for Scotland, Mr. John McCluskey, Q.C., said no investigative had come from anyone who had approached him privately.—(P.A.)

Cook admits he killed baby

Rory Connellan aged 23, a cook in the Royal Marines, who killed his baby daughter by fracturing her skull when her crying exasperated him, was jailed at Exeter Crown Court yesterday.

Mr Connellan denied murdering the child, aged four weeks, and his plea of guilty to manslaughter was accepted by the Crown.

Killings charge

Soldier David Nicholson, 17, was charged with killing his mother and her common-law husband. He was arrested after the bodies of Mrs Ann Nichol-son, 40, and William Kent, 44, were found in Washington, Tyne and Wear.

Army captain kept Irish Rangers private a prisoner

From Our Correspondent
Bristol

An Army captain who won the Military Cross in Belfast became so obsessed by the futile and aimless violence in Northern Ireland that he led a young Irish private, Wien was said at yesterday.

The strain showed in letters home from service in Belfast and he sounded quite desperate about the Birmingham public house bombings.

The third defence witness, said it to only was a colonial, Captain Ash was a most fessional and skilled soldier who was respected and liked this men. He was an impeccable performer, but a "loser", who bottled up his tensions.

Mr Colin Willis, for the prosecution, said Captain Ash led Ranger Costello into Battlebury Barracks, Battlebury, near Wiltshire, about August 29. He took him to the Old School, Upton, Scudamore, near Battlebury, Wiltshire, and there, tied up and imprisoned in a coalhouse, he locked in a bedroom for two days, Captain Ash lived in a house with two other soldiers, who were away at the...

For being held prisoner for two nights Ranger Costello was put in the car, with his hands tied, and blindfolded, and driven, across the Severn Bridge to Builth Wells, where Captain Ash drove up a metalled road and along a grass

---

PARAS ACCUSED OF BOMBING COLONEL

Barracks blast looked like IRA

EXCLUSIVE by JOE GORROD

TWO paratroopers are facing a court martial after an alleged IRA-style bomb attack on their colonel's house in Northern Ireland.

The members of the crack 3rd Battalion Parachute Regiment whose Colonel-in-chief is Prince Charles - are alleged to have broken into their colonel's home at Holywood, County Down, and planted a bomb with an anonymous note to say that the 38-year-old commanding officer, Lt Col Hamish Fletcher, himself could be their next target. The Army-owned mansion at the head of officers' row in the 3rd Battalion, the Parachute Regiment base, had windows blown out and was damaged by fire in the blast.

After the note was found Military Police began a hunt for the culprits.

"Two soldiers are to be court martialled on charges of arson and burglary," said a spokesman at Army headquarters in Lisburn, Co Antrim.

The tough Scottish colonel with a reputation for fearless leadership has made no comment about the attack.

But one former Para officer said: "He is a man who drives himself and his soldiers hard, the prime example of a parachute commander.

Danger

"He won't let a thing like that affect his judgement."

Col Fletcher is a graduate of Sandhurst and Staff College, Camberley, who has soldiered with the regiment through most of its most dangerous assignments in Northern Ireland.

The 3rd Battalion has done over a dozen tours of duty in the Province.

The Paras are now on a three-year tour, accompanied by their families. In one of the quietest areas.

The bomb incident was never logged by the Army or reported to the RUC.

One detective based near the barracks said: "There's many a thing goes on in an Army camp that we never hear about."

Soldier who went berserk 'not unique'

Daily Telegraph Reporter

THE pressure on Trooper Maggs, who went berserk with a rifle in his Belfast barracks this week, killing one NCO and wounding another before he was himself shot dead by a colleague, "represents only the tip of the problem" facing soldiers on Northern Ireland duty, a psychiatrist said yesterday.

"Despite what the Army says, his case is by no means unique," Dr Michael Simpson, 34, who is giving up his post as consultant and senior lecturer in the department of Psychiatry at the Royal Free Hospital to take up an American appointment, claimed yesterday.

Dr Simpson, who is to be a professor at Temple University, Philadelphia, said his comments are based on research on other troops who had also served in Northern Ireland.

for not placing the names of Northern Ireland victims on memorials. And one can only speculate on the real reasons, be they a fear of reprisals from terrorists or a belief that the conflict in Ireland is not really a war (as one eminent contemporary politician was reported as saying of the Suez campaign in 1956: "This is not war, it is armed conflict" – then as now, it did not make the bullets less lethal or the dead come back to life).[78]

Oliver Stone, a Vietnam veteran, made a series of films about US involvement in Vietnam. In the *Guardian*, journalist Martin Woollacott wrote about Stone:

> This idea of an America fighting itself is at the heart of his vision of Vietnam. The corruption of American society, in his argument, was such that an immoral government started a bad war and a degenerate middle class pushed the burden of fighting it off on to the poor and the ignorant. They, in turn, filled with anger at the way in which they had been abused, turned their rage on the Vietnamese.[79]

Much of Stone's view of the US/Vietnam situation would find a echo in Britain's policy towards Northern Ireland. In 1976, as the casualties of the conflict increased, the journalist James Fenton reported a debate at Westminster; 'I had been intending to kick off with a description of Monday's Northern Ireland debate, which I had imagined would be a dramatic affair. It was not a dramatic affair. The heat was off with a vengeance, and the turn out was low. An average of 20 sprawling MPs graced the Labour benches. By the time Sir Nigel Fisher had spoken this number was considerably reduced.' Fenton continued:

> Sir Nigel's analysis will give some idea of the level of political discussion:
> 'I cannot help feeling that the basic position of the Ulster Unionists in opposing any coalition is unhelpful and uncompromising. I accept that they have a logical democratic argument, but it has never been possible to apply logic to the reactions of Ireland – or of women! Emotions matter much more. Rex Harrison in My Fair Lady bewailed: "Why can't a woman be more like a man?" But they are not. It is just as unreal to demand that the Irish should be treated in the same way as the more logical English. I know this on both counts because I am married to an Ulster woman.'

Shortly afterwards the Liberal spokesman, Mr. Alan Beith, addressed slightly fewer than five inert, somnolent, socialist bodies.

... The debate was a triumph of consensus. There were no shouts of 'Resign' or cries of 'Withdraw', no wild cheers, no outraged interventions from the back benches. There was no division. From time to time a murmur of 'Hear, hear' wafted up to the packed galleries from the sparsely populated floor, but it was not a distinct 'Hear, hear', more a sort of 'Nyurdle, nyurdle', as if some enormous stomach was dealing with an enormous meal. It was an occasion for congratulations, six and a half hours of monotonous backslapping.[80]

Britain's political parties prided themselves on their 'bipartisanship' on Northern Ireland. This meant supporting and not criticising the ruling party's policy, a convention that led to a puerile level of discussions at Westminster about the problem. A few brave MPs questioned the Government's policy. Invariably, they were attacked by their own party bosses and other establishment voices, and were vilified by the media.

When the war refused to go away, most MPs toed the government line. Ex-Tory MP Matthew Parris wrote about his time in Westminster in the *Spectator* magazine: 'In seven years as a government backbencher I do not think I encountered more than a handful of MPs on either side who cared much what happened to Ulster. ... Most of the rest of us went along, more or less, with the policy of Her Majesty's Government, whatever that was – "not giving in to the men of violence" or something. But we tended to find, when Ireland was debated, that we had other things to do.' Parris continued:

> Plainly there was something amiss, not in Ireland – we knew something was amiss there – but here on the mainland. Here was a problem towards whose solution we were voting enormous sums and sending soldiers to die, and somehow we couldn't focus on it.
>
> ... I came to the view that if our Leader, Mrs Thatcher, had announced it as her opinion that Ulster must make its own way, there were around 50 colleagues who would protest, 50 who would bite their lips, and more than 200 who would confess it was what they had always thought but never liked to say. I stick to that assessment now.

I also concluded that nobody, including me, was going to be the first to voice such thoughts.

And so it was that, though from the day I entered Parliament I never had the slightest doubt that Britain both must and eventually will disengage from Ulster, I never said so.[81]

While the politicians shirked their responsibilities for the ongoing conflict, it was left to Britain's front line – young soldiers, often still in their teens – to keep the lid on the 'troubles'. It is hardly surprising that many of those troops felt bitter and resentful:

> Just as the American soldiers in Vietnam used to divide their existence between 'the Nam' and 'the World' so do the British soldiers in Ulster, with only the world outside seeming real while they lead a surrealistic existence in an unreal world punctured by the brutal reality of bombs and bullets.
>
> They feel that the people outside cannot understand this strange world of theirs and they feel cut off, forgotten. The impression they have is of people in safe England, so very close, watching their television sets, seeing the explosions and the bodies, saying, 'How terrible', and then turning to something really interesting like the price of petrol.[82]

In 1979, after Trooper Edward Maggs had cracked up in a Belfast army base and been shot dead by his fellow soldiers, his father, Douglas Maggs, talked to a London newspaper about his son's tours of duty in Northern Ireland:

> If only he had deserted everything would have been fine. Instead he stayed on and tried to face it. Nine out of 10 men out there must feel as he did. But he was the one to crack – when he had a gun in his hand. The reason for him leaving the Army he loved so much was that he could not face service in Northern Ireland.
>
> He dreaded going back there, but it wasn't just the mere fact that he was in danger. It was the fact that everyone is your enemy out there. No one wants you there – it's a lost cause like Vietnam. There is no end in sight.[83]

Who Guards the Guards?

At the end of the nineteenth century, Rudyard Kipling wrote the poem

'Tommy' from a soldier's point of view:

> I went into a public-'ouse to get a pint o' beer,
> The publican 'e up an' sez, 'We serve no red-coats here'.
> The girls be'ind the bar they laughed an' giggled fit to die,
> I out into the street again an' to myself sez I:
> O it's Tommy this, an' Tommy that, an' 'Tommy, go away';
> But it's 'Thank you, Mister Atkins', when the band begins to play.

> Yes, makin' mock o' uniforms that guard you while you sleep,
> Is cheaper than them uniforms, an' they're starvation cheap;
> An' hustlin' drunken soldiers when they're goin' large a bit,
> Is five times better business than paradin' in full kit.
> Then it's Tommy this, an' Tommy that, an'
> 'Tommy 'ow's yer soul?'
> But it's 'Thin red line of 'eroes' when the drums begin to roll.

Kipling was trying to highlight the ambivalent attitude many British people have towards their soldiers. In 1942, George Orwell wrote an essay about Rudyard Kipling as 'the prophet of British imperialism in its expansionist phase'. After attacking Kipling's jingoistic pro-imperialism, Orwell made the following observation; 'We all live by robbing Asiatic coolies, and those of us who are "enlightened" all maintain that those coolies ought to be set free; but our standard of living, and hence our "enlightenment", demands that the robbery shall continue.' Orwell then wrote:

> A humanitarian is always a hypocrite, and Kipling's understanding of
> this is perhaps the central secret of his power to create telling phrases. It
> would be difficult to hit off the one-eyed pacifism of the English in fewer
> words than in the phrase, 'making mock of uniforms that guard you while
> you sleep'. It is true that Kipling does not understand the economic aspects
> of the relationship between the highbrow and the Blimp. He does not see that
> the map is painted red chiefly in order that the coolie may be exploited.

Instead of the coolie he sees the Indian Civil Servant; but even on that plane his grasp of function, of who protects whom, is very sound. He sees clearly that men can only be highly civilised while other men, inevitably less civilised, are there to guard and feed them.[84]

The Empire, won on the point of soldiers' bayonets, was largely a money-making concern. While fortunes were made by British businessmen, all the British people benefited – most, however, to a much lesser extent – by the exploitation of natural resources and native labour.

The more recent wars at the rundown of Empire were about preserving – or at least keeping safe – British economic and strategic interests in the remnants of its Empire. Events in places like Malaya, Kenya, Cyprus and Aden, where British troops killed and were killed, constitute a hidden history to most British people. Northern Ireland was no exception; people expressed shock and horror about the violence, but said they did not understand what was happening, except that a series of shocking and disturbing incidents occurred 'over there', which sometimes spilled over onto British streets. That is how the conflict impinged on our consciousness. The media presented us with isolated events, totally incomprehensible because they were never presented in any historical or contemporary context.

The writer and playwright John Arden spent his period of National Service in the army a few years after the end of the Second World War. Later, in the early 1970s he encountered some soldiers during a journey: 'I travelled recently on the Irish Mail train from Euston to Liverpool. In the long open carriage was a group of very young "skinhead" soldiers, in full battle-gear, on their way to the Belfast ferry.' Arden continued:

> Nearly every passenger in that carriage was obviously Irish, from their speech. The soldiers sat in a mute savage huddle, their eyes twitching to follow the movements of each man who passed them on the way to the toilet or the buffet-car. For them, it was clear, the Falls Road began in Euston Square. I have said these boys were 'skinheads': their haircuts were civilian and cultic, even though they wore uniform. What is a 'skinhead' but the most alienated and rancorous product of our present state of industrial

opportunism compounded by induced unemployment? The rejects join the Army; already disturbed, they are inducted into an already lunatic system.[85]

Perhaps, the best insight into how these soldiers felt and acted in Northern Ireland comes from veterans who have written about their exploits. A F N Clarke served with the Paras as a private, as a NCO and as a commissioned officer from 1971 to 1978. In his book *Contact*, he describes a typical Para unit, inside a Wild West type army fort situated in a staunchly nationalist area of west Belfast:

As time drags on, the whole camp is praying for a contact. For an opportunity to shoot at anything on the street, pump lead into any living thing and watch the blood flow. Toms [soldiers] sitting in their overcrowded rooms putting more powder into baton rounds to give them more poke; some insert pins and broken razor blades into the rubber rounds. Buckshee rounds have the heads filed down for a dum-dum effect, naughty, naughty, but who's to know when there are so many spare rounds of ammunition floating about. Lead-filled truncheons, magnum revolvers, one bloke has even got a Bowie knife. Most of the NCOs and officers are aware that these things are around and if they aren't, then they shouldn't be doing the job. We have spent months and years training, learning from pamphlets called Shoot to Kill, Fighting in Built-up Areas and others. So now, we're let loose on the streets trained to the eyeballs, waiting for a suitable opportunity to let everything rip.[86]

This view of the soldiers hardly accords with the Westminster politicians' description of 'our boys' as a 'peacekeeping force'. Clarke's recollections are paralleled in another book, *Shoot To Kill*, by Michael Asher, who also outlines his experiences in the Parachute Regiment. In graphic detail Asher tells about his training and his tours of duty in Northern Ireland, outlining the tension and the fights that break out between soldiers in this situation. He describes the extremes that training, conditioning and alienation can bring out in some soldiers:

One group of soldiers would hold so-called 'gunge' contests. They sat round in a circle and tried to outdo each other in acts of gross obscenity, like eating shit and drinking urine. During house searches they vented their anger on their victims, smashing down doors and breaking up furniture,

A sniper's view — an army rifleman surveys a Belfast street

PEER'S VIET 'SON' IN SUICIDE AFTER ARMY RACE TAUNTS

By VICTOR CHAPPLE

A PEER'S "son" shot himself through the heart because of bullying by racist squaddies, a friend said yesterday.

Phuoc Ky Ennals, 22, turned an SA-80 rifle on himself after bigots with the Royal Green Jackets allegedly hurled him into a freezing river.

The Vietnamese orphan, who was given a home by former

Labour Cabinet Minister Lord Ennals, enlisted only last year.

But his hopes of a bright career were dashed when he became the target of racist thugs, his soldier pal claimed.

Exercise

He finally cracked and took his own [life] while on a training exercise [near a] bridge on the Brec[on Beacons] Mid-Wales.

"But he was right. [He] was fit and had [been] and [was] bullied on[...]

Tragic... orphan Phuoc

Rifle fired into heart

Caring... Lord Ennals

DAILY TELE 27-10-87

Marine jailed for drunken assaults in fancy dress

A Royal Marine who attacked six people, including two women, in a drunken rampage while wearing fancy dress of a red dress and black stockings, was jailed for two years at Exeter Crown Court yesterday.

Robert Harwood, 21, who was based at Lympstone, Devon, was on bail for attacking a police officer and another man when the assaults took place. He hit one of the women so hard he broke her jaw, and his other victims were left battered and bruised in the street.

THE DAILY TELEGRAPH, TUESDAY, APRIL 19, 1988

Undercover police exposed violence in Para's Army'

A [PARA]TROOPER was accused yesterday of [...] alleged soccer hooligans. The group [...] known as Para's Army, [...]men in a four-month under[...] named Wild Boar, a court was [...]

[...]d three [...]med false [...]anged their [...] they could [...]orters.

[...] man had his [...]ey all grew [...]wn Court

[...] conspiring [...]ray dur[...]ssion.

[...] prosecut[...] met in [...]centre black [...]police black [...] opposing fans.

[...]alleged former para[...]d Brown, 26, of Lid[...] Leeds, was the [...]organiser. He said [...]named Para, he [...]ed Para's Army [...]essed with food

disorder and all willingly took part in it."

He claimed a gang of 20 tried to incite people to fight in Lichfield en route to a game against West Bromwich Albion in December 1986. "They were chanting: 'We are Leeds' and 'Come on Birmingham Bastards' to the horror of people in the town centre, who were obviously disturbed," he said.

Guards' hold-up

Two Coldstream Guardsmen who robbed a building society because they were dissatisfied with their pay were each sent to a young offenders' institution for seven years at Plymouth Crown Court. Dale Watkins and Michael Lund Larsen, both 20, of the 2nd Battalion Coldstream Guards, pleaded guilty to robbing the Yorkshire Building Society branch in Dart[...]

TODAY 20-OCT 92

RAPIST KILLED MOTHER WHILE CHILDREN SLEP[T]

by NICK CRAVEN

TWO young girls lay asleep in their beds as a convicted rapist assaulted their mother in the next room then kidnapped her.

Crazed ex-soldier William O'Donnell broke into neighbour Adele James's home and stashed her underwear with an 8in carving knife.

While her children, aged seven and five, slept, he forced Mrs James, 21, to get dressed and drive her VW Polo to a remote cliff path a mile away.

Former Black Watch squaddie O'Donnell then grabbed the handcleaver with a piece of cord and as Adele put up a brave fight he pulled her by her belt towards the sea.

While she was still alive, O'Donnell, 31, dragged her into the water to drown. Her body was f[ound...]

Ex-sol[dier had] string of sex attac[ks]

Beer glas[s in] man's fac[e]

by Suzy Gibson, Court Staff

A SOLDIER on home leave smashed a beer glass into a man's face in a Leicester nightclub, a court heard.

Mark Chadwick (27), a private in the Parachute Regiment, grabbed hold of the victim — who accidentally bumped into him — and threatened: "Knock me again and I will kill you."

Then he broke the glass on Mr Darren Benson's head, causing a gash which needed six stitches, said Mr Mark Cursham, prosecuting.

£500 compensation

Chadwick, described as an "exemplary" soldier, currently on active duty in Northern Ireland, pleaded guilty to wounding 22-year-old Mr Benson, of New Parks, Leicester, in Braunigan's nightclub, Charchgate, in January.

At Leicester Crown Court, Judge Brian Appleby QC ordered Chadwick to pay his victim £500 compensation, with £150 court costs, and imposed a 12-month conditional discharge.

He told the defendant: "There are wholly exceptional circumstances. Normally, it would have been immediate imprisonment.

'Silly you[...]

"But this is so [...] you. What a silly [...] nearly throwing [...] the army."

Army represen[...] Lorimer told the co[...] would be discharged [...] received a custodial sen[...]

He described the [...] "good and exemplar[...] added: "We would lose [...] trained soldier. We [...]

04/7/[...]

GULF SOLDIERS GET THE BOOT

By ALAN GULLAN[...]

THREE Gulf War [S]cots have been [bo]oted out of the [a]rmy on drugs charges.

They are thought to have used cannabis when they were stationed in Germany.

Colchester's notorious Glasshouse Arnott got se[...] months. The sentence and the dismissal [...] all three from[...] service are subject [...] confirmation.

when they return to Britain.

But they are not likely to be kicked out of the Army.

The Kent-based regiment recruits mainly from London and the [...]

SQUADDIE HIGH ON ACID SMASHED UP BARRACKS

By JOHN HICKS and TOM MERRIN

A YOUNG soldier sparked a major Army drugs investigation after going berserk in his Ulster barracks, it was revealed yesterday.

He smashed windows while high on an LSD "acid trip." The soldier, from the 3rd Battalion of the Queen's Regiment, was arrested following his rampage at Aldergrove barracks 15 miles from Belfast.

He named his pusher and told senior officers about an extensive drugs ring.

Ten soldiers were arrested and are being held in military custody. "He dropped everybody in it," said a relative of one arrested squaddie.

10 soldiers held as Army probes Ulster drugs ring

kicking and rifle-butting anyone who resisted, making lewd suggestions to the women of the house and threatening the children.

...The circumstances of our training, coupled with the peculiar nature of our existence in Northern Ireland – a blend of boredom, frustration and occasional terror – turned us into savages. We begged and prayed for a chance to fight, to smash, to kill, to destroy: we were fire-eating berserkers, a hurricane of human brutality ready to burst forth on anyone or anything that stood in our way. We were unreligious, apolitical and remorseless, a caste of warrior-janizaries who worshipped at the high-altar of violence and wanted nothing more.[87]

The soldiers were intensely trained and indoctrinated for their tours of duty. From these descriptions we can see that, once in Northern Ireland, they were often hyped-up, aggressive time bombs, ready to explode into action and violence at any minute.

While we slept, these were the uniforms who guarded us – or at least maintained our establishment's hold on Northern Ireland. In Rome in 100AD, Juvenal asked the question: 'Quis custodiet ipsos custodes?' – 'Who guards the guards?' After we learn something about the actions of our soldiers in Northern Ireland and other conflicts, and see what happened to some of these veterans afterwards, perhaps we need to ask the same question about our army and our guards?

No doubt, some of the recruits who ended up on tours of duty in Northern Ireland had been among those youths on the football terraces who had taunted the police about Harry Roberts. They had followed him into the organisation that would teach them how to kill and the wars that would brutalize them. Now, like Roberts and Neilson and like many Vietnam veterans in the USA, some of Britain's soldiers have brought their violence home from Northern Ireland.

The Corporals' War

In 1990 I received a letter from Frankland maximum security prison in Durham from a category 'A' prisoner who was serving a life sentence for murder.

The writer, ex-soldier Jimmy Johnson, had served two tours of duty with the Royal Tank Regiment in Northern Ireland in the early 1970s. Johnson had been aware that his service in Ireland had changed him, but could not work out how or why till a chance meeting in prison. He made friends with a doctor, also serving a long sentence, who kept asking the ex-soldier about his tours of duty and the army preparation and training before them.

Then one day the doctor said that he thought Jimmy was probably suffering from PTSD. Not having heard about this condition before, a mystified Johnson shrugged his shoulders and asked the doctor what he was on about. The doctor explained by saying that from what Jimmy had told him it was obvious that the soldiers were wound up before a tour of duty and that the situation, once there, probably wound them up even more. The doctor added that it was apparent that there was no process for winding down afterwards. Some soldiers would no doubt be unaffected – others, like Jimmy, might leave Northern Ireland, but Northern Ireland would never leave them.

At that moment Johnson was not sure what to think, but the more he thought about his army service and his life after, the more he believed that the doctor might be right. In different prisons Jimmy had met many other ex-soldiers, almost all of whom had served tours of duty in Northern Ireland. Since leaving the army, most had followed a similar path to Jimmy – which had led them to prison also.

Desperate for help, Jimmy wrote to the MoD and to a now high-ranking officer he had served with. But he received noncommittal replies that were little more than polite brush-offs. Jimmy was also reading anything he could get his hands on that might give him a further understanding of his situation, and by chance came across a copy of my novel ... *last night another soldier* ... . Realising that as an ex-soldier I might understand, Jimmy wrote to me asking for assistance in taking up this issue:

> I have served in the army for ten years, 14 months in Aden (1965-1966) and a 4 month and a 12 month tour of duty in N. Ireland. ... Immediately after my 12 months tour in Ireland I bought myself out of the army, for family reasons.

Upon returning to civilian life I found I could not settle in or indeed adjust in any way. Although I had the offer of several steady and permanent jobs I simply could not cope. My marriage which had been under great strain whilst I was in Ireland now fell apart.

After that it was all downhill and within a mere four months of leaving the army, and my chosen career, I found myself in prison with a long sentence, hence the address. Once in prison I was surprised to find quite a number of ex-soldiers and N. Ireland veterans as fellow inmates. A much higher percentage I would suspect than average for any other profession.

This has set me to thinking of the American experience in Viet-Nam and the major adjustment problems their veterans have had upon their return, also the more recent but similar problems the Russians have experienced with their vets from Afghanistan. Now it really would be too much to believe that the British Soldier had come unscathed through 20 years of stress and trauma ...

Now the Americans have made no secret of their findings and problems, nor indeed have the Russians. But from us the British there is a total deafening silence. Consequently I would greatly appreciate any comment or opinion you might have on this whole aspect of what might best be described as post N. Ireland Trauma.[88]

In military circles, Northern Ireland was often referred to as the 'corporals' war'. Because, in the main, it was the corporals who commanded the patrols that ventured out into the 'Indian country' of nationalist areas. In Frankland prison, ex-corporal and Northern Ireland veteran Jimmy Johnson wrote out the history of his time in the army and what that had led to. Called *Their Country's Reward*, Jimmy's manuscript contains graphic accounts of his training and tours of duty in Northern Ireland. As 'tankies', Jimmy's unit needed special training for Northern Ireland and a fiercesome staff-sergeant from the Welsh Guards was allocated to train them. This included intensive weapons firing drill, riot training with other soldiers as the rioters, and practice on the close-quarter combat range at Sennelarger. Called 'Tin City' by the soldiers, the range was like a little bit of Northern Ireland:

On arrival there you could not see anything from the outside because of a wall of corrugated metal. Sheets of this went the whole way round the range. There was a small doorway built into this wall which was the only way in for us. On entering we were led into a small room then given a briefing.

My men were then informed that once we were sent through another door (which led onto the range) we would be on 'foot patrol' in an area of Belfast.

... I got the shock of my life for when we came through the doorway, I was standing in a street. The street was just like any street in England! ... Then from a 'public house' which was situated on a street corner, we could hear the sounds of IRA Republican Rebel songs, as if the customers in the bar were actually singing these songs.

Shortly after moving down the street on our patrol we heard the sounds of dustbin-lids being banged together. The dustbin-lids were part of an 'early warning system' used in the Catholic housing estates to warn the residents that 'The Brits' were on their estate. It also warned the Army patrols to expect Snipers – Bombs – Riots or whatever else could happen. Very soon after the lid banging stopped, the brickwork just above my head exploded. Bits of stone hit me in the face, but I didn't have time to think about that, I was already diving down to the floor and finding what cover I could ...[89]

Toughness and aggression was instilled into the men as well as the other training drills. Once in Northern Ireland the soldiers were anxious to put what they had learned into practice and often went looking for 'aggro'. Based at Lurgan, Jimmy often took his patrols into the hostile Kilwilkie estate; 'When I first took my section on a mobile patrol through this estate – we loved it! We had never experienced anything like it before – the whole estate hated the Brits! The Paddies on this estate would always greet us with anything they could throw at us – even gunmen! Yet every time I took a mobile patrol out – my men would want to go into the Kilwilkie estate – this is where the aggro is!'[90] The conflict was often fierce, with no quarter asked for, or given, by either side. In riots, the soldiers had official equipment like rubber bullets and batons. But, if the fighting got to close

He Kept Our Boys Out Of Northern Ireland

Produced in the early 70s, this was the American anti-Vietnam war movement's ironic comment on Britain's war in Ireland

DAILY Mirror

Monday, February 26, 1979   8p

Deserter dies in raid on house

A MAN ARMY deserter has died after a couple made a citizen's arrest when he tried to break into their home.

Anthony Desmond, 18, was overpowered. Later an off duty policeman helped restrain him as he shouted: "Let me go, I don't want to go back to Ulster."

ULSTER VICTIM WAS 'SOLDIER'

A MAN believed to be a British soldier was at the centre of a death riddle in the Irish Republic yesterday.

He was found dying south of the border and a revolver was lying nearby. He had been shot through the head.

The drama began shortly after dawn. People living in the town of Killymarley heard a single shot.

A number of men on their way to work at a

ARMY SHOOTS CRAZED SOLDIE[R]

Two die in gun battle at barracks

ARMY marksmen killed one of their fellow soldiers yesterday when he went berserk with a rifle.

The order to gun down 20-year-old Edward Maggs came after he shot two NCOs.

One of them, Quartermaster Corporal John Tucker, 34, shot from his wounds.

Doctors were fighting last night to save the life of the other victim, 26-year-old Lance Corporal David Melhe.

Wildly

An Army spokesman said: "They both acted in the line of course."

MAGGS: Killed after he refused to su[rrender]

By JOHN HICKS and PETER

Soldier shooting riddle

A RMY top brass were last night investigating the shooting of a Scots soldier at a firing range.

Gulf War veteran David Ellis, 24, had just completed an exercise at Oakington near Cambridge on Friday when he was hit.

Royal Highland Fusilier David, from Glasgow, was rushed to Colchester General Hospital where his condition is "satisfactory".

Fusilier Ellis had been due to receive his Gulf War medal today along with the rest of his regiment.

Bosnia trauma 'caused army suicide'

Geoffrey Gibbs

A SOLDIER hanged himself because of his traumatic experiences during tours of duty in Bosnia and Northern Ireland, his mother claimed yesterday. Elaine Burrington said the army seemed not to have listened to her pleas that Wayne Passmore, aged 27, needed help.

Army pair's roof demo

T WO soldiers staged an amazing rooftop mutiny at an Army base in Ulster.

The pair clambered up during the night at Ebrington Barracks in Londonderry.

And they refused to budge until their demands were met.

A number of plastic bullets are believed to have been fired in the direction of the sergeants' mess.

Pistol terror soldier jailed

A SCOTS Guard who terrorised a barracks thought he was still in the Falklands.

Lance-Sergeant Alex Findlay fired a pistol bullet through a TV set.

Then he threatened to kill two soldiers and held two more at gunpoint.

A court martial at Regent's Park Barracks, London, was told 30-year-old Findlay was

Brit soldier's death probe

● A TEENAGE British soldier with NATO's force in Bosnia died of gunshot wounds yesterday.

Officials probing the death of Aled Jones, 18, from Pwllheli, North Wales, don't suspect crime or a sniper shot.

Ulster deaths probe

T HE mystery deaths of two young soldiers in Ulster were being investigated by Army chiefs yesterday, although police suspected no crime.

Gunner Darren Oldfield, 18, died after being found shot in the head at a base in South Armagh, while earlier Private Jonathan Edmunds, 22, was said to have died from natural causes during training.

Squaddie in crazed shoot-out

A BRITISH soldier went berserk and opened fire at mourners outside bomber Thomas Begley's Belfast home yesterday.

And a leading member of the republican movement was seriously injured.

quarters, the squaddies often used their own 'personal' weapons, as Jimmy recounts:

> I spotted two men who were coming at me from the crowd (The only
> defence I could use in this situation was to open fire with a rubber bullet. I
> had the baton gun loaded and ready to fire). The first of these men was only a
> few feet from me and his mate was behind him. I fired at the man who was
> nearly upon me. The explosion of the rubber bullet being fired seemed
> deafening in the street. I couldn't see anything because of the smoke from the
> rubber bullet being fired. Then there were screams from the women and
> children and shouts from the men. I could now see my men and the crowd
> fighting hand to hand with each other. The crowd had their sticks and other
> weapons and so did my men (We never used the official baton stick, they
> were useless, they broke too easily. My men had their own personal weapons;
> baseball bats, hammers, lead pipes – anything that wouldn't break easily.
> These weapons were passed on from other soldiers, after their tour of duty
> had finished). I carried a black-jack cosh that fitted in my combat trousers
> easily. But I didn't use that, I had the baton gun in my hand and I was now
> looking for the other man.[91]

Afterwards, two incidents in particular would continue to haunt Jimmy from the conflict. In the first, Jimmy had rescued a woman from an underground toilet in Lurgan after a bomb explosion. There was thought to have been another bomb in the area, but Jimmy and two of his men refused to leave till they had dug out the woman and carried her to the waiting medical team. The woman reminded Jimmy of his wife and he begged the medics to save her, but she died from her horrendous injuries. For his bravery, Jimmy was 'mentioned in dispatches', his regiment's highest honour since the Korean war.

The second incident had occurred in the middle of a riot. During fierce fighting between Jimmy's men and the local people, a man had crept up behind a soldier and thrown a bucket of paint over him. Jimmy, in a blind rage, chased the man through the lines of fighting into the nationalist estate. Jimmy, still very angry but now also fearful because of his isolated location, chased the man into the kitchen of a house. There, as another resident sat at a table eating a meal, Jimmy caught his quarry trying to escape through a window. Using the rubber-bullet gun he had been carrying, Jimmy battered the man into submission; 'I hit the bloke with the rubber-bullet gun. I was trying to get him down on the floor, but he wouldn't go down. I hit him three or four times on the head. Blood spurted out of his head like an oil-well – I couldn't stop, I was panicking and he wouldn't go down'.[92]

Jimmy eventually stopped when another soldier entered the room and yelled at him, 'Jimmy, he's had enough.' In the USA, the volume of PTSD among Vietnam veterans suggests that the nature of the conflict and the violence that soldiers have inflicted play a large part in this condition occurring:

> ... it was not merely the exposure to death but rather the participation in meaningless acts of malicious destruction that rendered men most vulnerable to lasting psychological damage. In one study of Vietnam veterans, about 20 percent of the men admitted to having witnessed atrocities during their tour of duty in Vietnam, and another 9 percent acknowledged personally committing atrocities. Years after their return from the war, the most symptomatic men were those who had witnessed or participated in abusive violence. Confirming these findings, another study of Vietnam veterans found that every one of the men who acknowledged participating in atrocities had post-traumatic stress disorder more than a decade after the end of the war.[93]

After buying himself out of the army, Jimmy Johnson found he 'could not handle Civvy Street.' Suffering from nightmares and tension he began to drink heavily, and, drifting from job to job, his marriage started to disintegrate. One day near Middlesbrough, Jimmy killed a security guard, who was a former workmate:

> Johnson remembers being offered a lift by the guard. He says: 'I've a vague recollection of kids playing on the side of the road. All I remember is a crash on the side of the van. I think the kids had thrown something at it. The next thing I remember is running, I was carrying Keith (his victim). I dropped him down, I battered him with a pole, I must have hit him three or four times.'
>
> ... He says that when attacking his victim he was thinking about 'hitting

the bloke in Northern Ireland'.[94]

Jimmy Johnson pleaded guilty to murder and served nine years in jail. He was released on licence in 1983. Eighteen months later, Jimmy killed for a second time, while doing some building work at his victim's home in Blackburn:

> Johnson smashed the skull of Robin Harwood, 41, a school laboratory technician, hitting him six times with a lump hammer.
>
> ... He was again sentenced to life, this time with a recommendation that he serve a minimum of 30 years ...
>
> Johnson was apparently convinced he was suffering from PTSD by a wife-killing doctor who shared his cell. His case was taken up by criminal lawyer Stephen Sullivan, who believed Johnson had grounds for an appeal.
>
> In January and May 1994, Johnson was examined by Dr Morgan O'Connell, a former consultant psychiatrist with the Royal Navy, who believes the ex-soldier carried out both murders while 'in a state of detachment or flashback to conditions of severe stress whilst serving in Northern Ireland'.
>
> Johnson's lawyers have been granted a full legal aid certificate ...
>
> Johnson's legal team will argue that he should have been able to plead guilty to manslaughter on the grounds of diminished responsibility. But as the illness [PTSD] was recognised only in the mid-1980s, they will claim he had no option but to plead guilty to murder.[95]

In courts in the USA after PTSD had been officially recognised, it became permissible for Vietnam veterans diagnosed as suffering from this condition to use it as a mitigating circumstance. There have been a few cases of British soldiers being convicted of killings while serving in Northern Ireland. These soldiers, like paratrooper Lee Clegg, usually received sympathetic treatment in British courts and the media. Often, there were establishment-led campaigns to obtain their release. Similarly, serving soldiers on trial for serious offences committed in Britain are usually supported by the army, who will make appeals on their behalf.

For most ex-soldiers, however, things are different. There is often no help for them from their old regiment or the MoD and no sympathy from establishment elements. As soon as they leave the army, they find they are on their own. Families of British soldiers returning from Ireland are devastated when their sons and husbands crack up, or start acting out of character. Marriages and other relationships often break down, leaving many ex-soldiers to face their torment on their own. Jimmy Johnson's father tried to get some answers from the politicians after his son had ended up in jail:

> It was at HMP Wakefield that my father informed me he had been to see Barbara Castle MP, about me ...
>
> He told Barbara Castle, "That there was something wrong because one minute they wanted to pin medals on my chest, then 12 months later they were locking me up for life!" ...
>
> A few weeks later Barbara Castle MP called my father and sister down to her surgery, she told them she had been sitting next to Mr Merlyn Rees MP (at the time Secretary of State for Northern Ireland) in the House of Commons. She remembered my father asking her about my case, so she mentioned it to Mr Rees. She told my father, when Mr Rees first replied to her question he must have been taken unawares, because the first words coming from Mr Rees were, "**I think the country would be shocked by the amount of soldiers coming out of Northern Ireland and finishing up in the prisons of the country!**" [my emphasis] He also mentioned about me pleading guilty – so there was nothing he could do.[96]

The War Comes Home

After receiving Johnson's letter from Frankland prison – and overcoming my initial scepticism – I gradually realised that Jimmy had highlighted a major hidden issue of the conflict. I then started to look for other examples of veterans, who, like Jimmy, had become involved in violent acts back in Britain after their return from tours of duty in Northern Ireland. After monitoring a few newspapers and a little bit of research, I was surprised at how quickly a file of cases could be built up.

The only reporting of these occurrences is when they appear as small and fragmented articles in newspapers. For a few seconds they draw our attention and we perhaps feel sorrow or anger, then we quickly move on to other news. The true picture only starts to emerge if we put a series of these incidents together. What follows are examples, taken from the pages of papers, where veterans have been involved in tragic and often violent incidents.

It is often the soldiers themselves who are in danger. Sometimes, they feel they can no longer bear their torment:

> A soldier hanged himself because of his traumatic experiences during tours of duty in Bosnia and Northern Ireland, his mother claimed yesterday.
>
> Elaine Burrington said the army seemed not to have listened to her pleas that Wayne Passmore, aged 27, needed help.
>
> Mrs Burrington, an auxiliary hospital nurse, discovered her son's body hanging at her Barnstaple home
>
> ... In a statement read to yesterday's inquest she said her son, a private in the Devon and Dorset Regiment, had told her of atrocities he had seen in Bosnia, including the dismembered bodies of children. He had also seen two colleagues shoot themselves dead in front of him and had come under bombardment while driving in convoy.
>
> Mrs Burrington said her son had served in Northern Ireland for six months and his experiences there had 'affected his life'.
>
> ... Mrs Burrington said she spoke of her concerns to an officer and a padre at his unit, saying her son needed counselling. But the officer had said he thought her son was trying to get out of the army.[97]

Sometimes, violence explodes at a veteran's home:

> A father killed his wife, teenage daughter and himself in a shotgun horror early yesterday.
>
> ... The triple tragedy was discovered when Barry Downes, 14, ran screaming from the family home in the fishing village of Portavogie, Co Down.
>
> Police then found the bodies of Stuart Downes, 41, his wife Elizabeth, 37, and 17-year-old daughter Joanne.
>
> ... Neighbours said Englishman Downes was a former soldier who had served in Ulster before moving from East Belfast and setting up a car restoring business.

Downes had been drinking before the shootings, according to neighbours.[98]

In other cases, a soldier takes desperate actions which can have tragic results:

An Army deserter has died after a couple made a citizen's arrest when he tried to break into their home.

Anthony Desmond, 18, was overpowered. Later an off duty policeman helped restrain him as he shouted: 'Let me go, I don't want to go back to Ulster'.

Desmond, of Castlemilk, Glasgow, was taken away by other officers. But later he was rushed to hospital where he was found to be dead.

The cause of death was 'traumatic asphyxiation'. ... Desmond's pregnant widow said: 'I can hardly believe what has happened ... He deserted ... while serving in Germany, simply because he did not want to serve in Ireland'.[99]

Often, the veterans cause harm to others they come in contact with. In 1990, at Lincoln central railway station, a civilian was to meet violence at the hands of an ex-para:

A frustrated commuter pushed a suicidal woman from a railway bridge because she was making him late.

The depressed 23-year-old had delayed trains for 40 minutes as she contemplated whether to end her life on the tracks 20ft below.

But before police could coax her down, Falklands veteran Ieuan Bullivant made her mind up for her.

The ex-para colour sergeant coolly put down his luggage, brushed past [police] officers and walked up the footbridge steps.

He shouted to the terrified woman: 'Either jump or get down', then pushed her onto the tracks.

The fall left Lorraine Briggs with two broken ankles, a fractured knee and a broken neck.

... Bullivant, 39, who went back down to platform 6, picked up his bags and continued waiting for his train, was arrested on the spot as his victim was rushed to hospital ...

... Bullivant, now a security guard ... received glowing references from

the army, where he served six tours of duty in Ulster and saw action in the
Falklands ...

He was jailed for 15 months after admitting inflicting grievous bodily
harm. The court was told it was doubtful Miss Briggs, still in hospital, would
make a complete recovery from her injuries.[100]

Local papers often carry coverage from court cases: In 1991, the *Leicester Mercury*
reported how a serving soldier on standby for the Gulf War took part in a violent
event on a Leicester street:

A soldier who could be called to serve in the Gulf at any time was part of a
gang who mugged a young man in a Leicester alleyway ...

Jason Lee Hill (20), a private with the 1st Royal Anglian Regiment based
in Colchester, was on leave when he and a gang of youths cornered Mr
Alkesh Vara.

... Finding he had only 30p in his pockets, they took his £180 gold chain.
Hill admitted his part in the robbery ...

Mr Willie Bach, defending, said Hill was described by the army as a
'model soldier'.

He had served in Northern Ireland and had come under fire while on
patrol there.

Mr Bach said: 'He is an exemplary soldier who has no previous
convictions, and the army still want him.'[101]

In 1993, the same paper told how a serving para, Mark Chadwick, had
assaulted another man in a Leicester pub:

A soldier on home leave smashed a beer glass into a man's face in a
Leicester nightclub, a court heard.

Mark Chadwick (27), a private in the Parachute Regiment, grabbed hold
of the victim – who accidentally bumped into him – and threatened: 'Knock
me again and I will kill you.'

Then he broke the glass on Mr Darren Benson's head, causing a gash
which needed six stitches ...

Chadwick, ... currently on active duty in Northern Ireland, pleaded
guilty to wounding 22-year-old Mr Benson ...

... Judge Brian Appleby QC ordered Chadwick to pay his victim £500 compensation, with £150 court costs, and imposed a 12-month conditional discharge.

He told the defendant: 'There are wholly exceptional circumstances. Normally, it would have been immediate imprisonment.

'But this is so out of character for you. What a silly young man you are, nearly throwing away a good career in the army.'

Army representative Major John Lorimer ... described the defendant as a 'good and exemplary soldier'.[102]

In 1997, the *Cambridge Evening News* reported how some soldiers carried out a violent attack on the city's streets:

Three soldiers who attacked a university student after a seven-hour drinking binge have been locked up.

The Oakington Barracks soldiers, who had just returned from a tour of duty in Northern Ireland, confronted the Sidney Sussex undergraduate in Bridge Street late at night. They chased him, pushed him to the ground and kicked him during an unprovoked attack. They then carried out a second attack as he made his way to the Baron of Beef pub, where he thought he would be safe.

... Judge John Sheerin said that although he could understand the stresses they were under in Northern Ireland, the incidents had 'sickening overtones'.[103]

In 1993, three soldiers were arrested after robbing a post office in Enfield, north London:

Three soldiers used terrorist tactics they witnessed in Northern Ireland to carry out a violent robbery campaign

... Mark Ayres, aged 19, Ian Tunks, 20, and Zenon Brown, 20, used imitation handguns and wore camouflage jackets and balaclavas. They raided a petrol station, held two motorists at gunpoint in Sevenoaks, Kent, and robbed a post office of nearly £6,000.

... The court heard the men had been traumatised in Ulster and may have been exhibiting post-traumatic stress syndrome.[104]

SOUTH LONDON PRESS, Friday, October 19th, 1990 15

Ex-SAS man torched home

A 'HARD drinking, hard working' former SAS soldier who torched his girlfriend's home in a drunken rage when he was told to move out.

John Russell (62), who served overseas with both the Special Air Service and the Parachute Regiment, received a suspended sentence at the Old Bailey for starting the blaze.

Earlier the court heard how relations between him and widow Valerie Ashmore (52), of Garratt Lane, Wandsworth, had soured over his endless drinking and she had asked him to leave.

But the building services manager 'made no effort' to go, the court heard on Monday.

When her son-in-law threatened to change the locks on June 17 last year, Russell sprinkled petrol in every room and then set the place alight.

As flames swept through the terraced house, Russell had a couple of drinks calmly by then gave himself up to police station.

He told officers, "I out of spite. No-one tell what to do."

Jailed Para faces sack on assault conviction

A PARATROOPER and his friend who brutally punched and kicked a youth after an argument over a taxi have both been sent to a young offenders' institution for 13 months.

Southwark Crown Court heard that 6'6" tall Brett Spence now faced being thrown out of the Parachute Regiment.

Assistant Recorder Mr Michael Hucker was told Spence would be

---

SAS BEAST BEATS JAIL

A TERRIFIED woman jumped from a bedroom window breaking her ankle when ex-SAS man Peter Docherty forced his way in and ordered her to strip, a court heard yesterday.

Docherty, 33, escaped jail at Guildford Crown court after Judge Anthony Lewisohn praised his Army record.

Docherty, of Ash, Surrey, was cleared of burglary with intent to rape but found guilty of actual bodily harm, and given a nine-month suspended sentence.

Off-duty soldier headbutted 'birdwatcher he thought was a paramilitary'

A SOLDIER on leave head-butted a birdwatcher after mistaking him for a paramilitary when emerged from woods wearing camouflage gear and a balaclava, a court was told yesterday.

Royal Engineers sapper Andrew Davies, (21), who served in the Gulf War, "panicked" and head-butted Karl Lauford, (18), breaking his nose, Cardiff Crown Court heard.

He allegedly told police: "I was trained that terrorist attacks can come at any time — when

---

Sikh terrorism trial

Times 30/10/87

'Cut-price killer' guilty of shootings

By Mark Ellis

A former soldier called the "cut-price killer" be of willingness to sh

Mr Thomas J prosec

ing them in the head with a sawn-off shotgun.

...ton, Bedfordshire, president of the town's branch of the ...an Overseas Congress, ...essed more th ...ctors, wh

police o oth

Nose bitten off in brawl

...ght party

...Bowcott

...arged with causing grievous ...ly harm, a third with caus...actual bodily harm.

...spokesman said: ...oldiers were arrested. ...our were released on

...are on hand to see ...complaints will be

...inistry of Defence ...sman said it was a civil

● Two instructors at Shorncliffe Barracks, in Folkestone, Kent, have been reprimanded for ill-treating and assaulting young soldiers in the Junior Infantry Battalion stationed there.

Cases against three other instructors, investigated by the ...y's Special Investigation ...ch, are still being ...red.

...other instructors were

Court martial jails soldier and his

AN ARMY gun committed sex against girls was ja 10 years by a court at Catterick, North shire yesterday.

His wife, who conceal offences for 10 years, was for 18 months, she is thoug be the first civilian tri court martial in Kingdom.

Acting L/Bdr M den, 36, of the Royal admitted 18 charges, inc offences, against girls between seven and 17.

Mrs Mary Madden, 37, ad ted two charges of gross ind cency jointly with her husba and two other offences.

Madden was also order be dismissed with disgrace his regiment. The senten subject to confirmation.

'CRAZED SQUADDIE SHOT BULLY SARGE 7 TIMES'

22 JUN 1990

4 soldiers in drug inquiry still on run

By Jenny Shields

FOUR SCOTTISH soldiers who escaped from a high security camp while being questioned by military police over alleged drug abuse in Ulster were still on the run last night.

Five men, all members of the 1st Battalion, Black Watch, broke out of the camp at Bally Kinler, Co Down, on Monday night and made their way to Larne where they caught a ferry to Stranraer.

Police forces throughout Scotland were alerted and on Tuesday night one soldier was detained by Tayside police during a routine broad check.

A police spokesman at Dundee said yesterday that the man — who is not being named — was handed over to the military authorities.

Allegations of drug taking involving members of the Perth-based regiment surfaced last week.

An Army spokesman said yesterday: "Four soldiers who were helping military police with their investigations into allegations of drug abuse by members of the Black Watch are absent without leave. A fifth soldier who had also been absent without leave is back in custody.

"A number of other soldiers who are helping with inquiries have been confined to barracks."

─World Report─

DAILY EXPRESS Monday August 13 1990

Dr Tracy's with killer

A BRITISH woman doctor was recovering last night after a 24-hour kidnap ordeal.

Tracy Clark, 28, was snatched in West Germany by a soldier who shot dead two forestry workers.

For most of the time she was tied up.

But Tracy, a captain serving with the Rhine Army who

From JOHN ENGLAND in Bonn

recently won a prize for psychiatry, finally talked her captor into giving himself up.

She was kidnapped last Friday afternoon after advertising her Vauxhall Astra car for sale in a forces newspaper.

A soldier made an appointment for a test drive. Thirty minutes after leaving her base

at Bielefeld keys in the ig abandoned.

"The man his car to area in north British Arr Major David

"It was the forestry wor dead.

"But Tracy competent mis about being struck by the sergeant, and Ken McMahon, QC, prosecuting at Enniskillen Crown for work

---

A TEENAGE soldier "snapped"

when he was thumped in the face by a sergeant . . . and blasted his tormentor to death with a burst of gunfire, a court heard yesterday.

Private Jason Chilton loosed off a hail of 14 bullets. Seven of them smashed into Dean Oliver's head and chest and the 30-year-old sergeant died on the spot.

The violence was sparked by an earlier clash between Chilton and a lance-corporal, the jury was told.

The 19-year-old private defied an order from the NCO — and hit him. Two days afterwards Sergeant Oliver spoke to the squaddie about the row and took him behind a garage.

When Chilton came back his nose was bleeding and his eyes were swollen.

Fellow members of the First Staffordshire Regiment, who were on a tour of duty in Northern Ireland at the time, heard the sergeant warn Chilton not to lay his hands on any NCO again or he would "get the same".

Forget

Chilton later asked another lance-corporal at Fivemiletown, County Tyrone, what he could do about being struck by the sergeant, said Ken McMahon, QC, prosecuting at Enniskillen Crown Court.

thought was a joking way: "I'll kill him."

Sergeant Oliver, a father of two, was kneeling down making tea when the private opened fire, the court heard.

Neutral

Corporal Ian Radford said he was sitting at a table when he heard a burst of automatic fire and saw Chilton holding his gun in both hands.

"I looked in his face and I didn't see any surprise or fear," the corporal went on. "His face was neutral."

Chilton then threw down his gun and another private jumped on him.

Chilton, from Stoke on

Murder court told of soldier hit in the face

By PATRICK MULCHRONE

Soldier on Gulf standby in court

A SOLDIER who could be called to serve in the Gulf at any time was part of a gang who mugged a young man in a Leicester alleyway, a court was told.

Jason Lee Hill (20), a private with the 1st Royal Anglian Regiment based in Colchester, was on leave when he and a gang of youths cornered Mr Alkash Vara in an alleyway, off Glenfield Road, Leicester.

Two years before, a Northern Ireland veteran in Scotland had been jailed for two years for robbing a shop:

> Former soldier James Robertson tried to drown his horror memories of Northern Ireland in drink, a court heard yesterday.
>
> But after downing eighteen cans of lager and a bottle of vodka, he and another man robbed a shop using a fake firearm.
>
> ... Robert Anthony, defending, said Robertson had served five years in Ulster.
>
> He added: 'He witnessed the aftermath of a bomb attack in which an acquaintance was killed. That was the turning point in his life. That was when he turned to alcohol.'[105]

In 1994, the *Sun* published an 'OUR BOYS ARE CRACKING UP' series of stories, after a group of soldiers contacted them and gave the newspaper details of their problems:

> Squaddie Stephen Bitcon told last night how fighting terrorists in Ulster made him crack up.
>
> The Sun revealed yesterday how five soldiers have been sent home from the King's Own Royal Border Regiment after breaking under the strain of working 123 hours a week.
>
> Stephen, 22, was discharged from the regiment after beating up a taxi driver while on leave. A judge freed him blaming his crime on the stress of serving in Londonderry.
>
> Stephen said: 'Every night on patrol we had rocks and bottles thrown at us. I was hit in the face with a brick and had glass from a bottle hit me in the eye. The barracks are really cramped and have rats running around in them. At night there is nothing to do but drink.'
>
> Stephen, a private, said: 'I became what the soldiers call a stress-outer. When I got home on leave I just wanted to forget by drinking myself silly. I would drive around like a maniac hoping to crash so I wouldn't have to go back to Ireland.'[106]

The *Sun* was 'flooded with calls' from soldiers' relatives agreeing and adding to the information that the paper had printed. Many came from wives and mothers:

One soldier's wife revealed many husbands turned from caring fathers into monsters while serving in Northern Ireland.

She said: ' ... Many take speed to stay awake . This, with drink, makes them violent towards their wives.'

The gran of a young soldier who took speed to stay awake claimed his life was in ruins. She said: 'He's given up on life.'

A squaddie's mum told how her boy survived the Gulf War, then turned to drugs in Northern Ireland.

She said: 'He tried to smuggle drugs into England and was discharged. He is struggling for a job.'

One private said his best friend is awaiting court martial after cracking up and running amok with a gun.

He said: 'He flipped and fired nine rounds in the street.'

An ex-soldier saw five friends killed by a car bomb in Londonderry.

He said: 'No-one gave us counselling. A corporal was trapped, crying for help on his radio. He was threatened with loss of wages for not using correct radio procedure.'[107]

Of course, many ex-soldiers have settled back into life back home, seemingly unaffected by their service in conflict situations. Some even used their experiences to good effect in Civvy Street. Nigel Benn and Terry Marsh are ex-soldiers and Northern Ireland veterans who became world champion boxers. Both were fierce fighters who often overcame more skilful opponents by sheer aggression. In 1989, Nigel Benn, who was then the Commonwealth middleweight boxing champion, was asked if he ever felt afraid in the ring. He replied:

Christ, I remember the day we arrived in Ulster. All the Rambos in our regiment [1st Battalion Royal Regiment of Fusiliers] were loving it – they were crazy – they thought this was all some film, like. I knew it was no film. For every single moment I was there, for two whole bloody years, I was terrified, man, sheer terrified! Even today, man, when I hear a click, my ass hits the floor! I lost four of my best mates there, blown to bits, and I wonder now just what the hell it was all for. No, man, I have no fears in the ring, absolutely none at all. After two years crawling around Tyrone and South

Armagh, it don't frighten me none![108]

Nigel Benn and Terry Marsh had both left the army and Northern Ireland behind and gone on to find fame and fortune in the boxing ring. Many other veterans were not so fortunate. Benn, who liked a 'good tear-up', was so aggressive that many people thought he had something driving him. Perhaps it was the same thing that drove so many other Northern Ireland veterans into violence and jail. In 1994, the *Guardian* published an article which explained how 'Ex-soldiers are increasingly becoming involved in professional crime, according to police and probation officers and welfare workers':

... Some are using skills acquired in the army to carry out armed robberies with military precision.

...A probation officer with four former soldiers serving sentences for armed robbery as clients, says many ex-servicemen are unprepared for civilian life.

Speaking of an ex-soldier serving a three-year sentence for robbery, she said: 'No-one had prepared him for the fact that there were no jobs around. He was used to a regular salary and had a wife and child to support. They come out with terrific expectations and then find out that life isn't like that.'

Three other former soldiers who had served in Northern Ireland are now serving six-year sentences for the armed robbery of a post office. They had suffered traumas from their experiences in Northern Ireland, she said, but had received no counselling.[109]

A typical example of this type of ex-soldier involvement in crime had occurred in Glasgow two years earlier:

A former soldier who turned to crime was yesterday jailed for 10 years.

The High Court in Glasgow heard Robert Smith, 39, had endured harrowing tours of duty in Ulster.

When he left the Army he suffered a personality change and chalked up an 'appalling record' of crime.[110]

Not all of the veterans featured in these examples will have been suffering from PTSD. Some, who became desensitised and brutalised by their training and tours of duty, have turned to crime in Civvy Street. Using their combat skills for personal gain. In the mid-1980s a gang, known as the Rambo Raiders carried out a series of robberies of Glasgow pubs. They were armed with sawn-off shotguns, a rifle and a revolver, and wore camouflage combat jackets with black and green hoods. The gang leader, ex-soldier Kenneth Ross who had served in Northern Ireland, was jailed for fifteen years:

> Kenneth Ross, a former soldier, was the leader of a gang of Rambo Raiders who terrorised Glasgow pubs in a 13-month robbery spree.
>
> ... Ross ... had been found guilty of nine charges of assault and robbery, fraud, possession of weapons, aiming a sawn-off shotgun at a detective with intent to murder him ...
>
> With him in the dock were: Donald MacDonald, 19, ... another former soldier, detained in a young offenders' institution for eight years on six assault and robbery charges ...
>
> ... In court yesterday the judge, Lord Cullen ... addressing both Ross and MacDonald, who had served in Ulster with their former regiment, The Queen's Own Highlanders ... said it was disheartening to find their Army skills had been put to such ill use in order to gain easy money ...
>
> ... Ethel Ross [Kenneth's mother] ... referring to the fact that her son would receive a long jail sentence ... added ... 'The Army has really changed him. You know ... they just give them guns and tell them to go out and shoot people.'[111]

In 1985 a serving soldier, William Ennis, was jailed for robberies in Belfast and Glasgow:

> A soldier who claimed he cracked under the strain of serving in Ulster was jailed for four years yesterday.
>
> Royal Highland Fusilier William Ennis, 21, robbed a building society in Glasgow while on leave.
>
> ... Ennis admitted assaulting assistants Helen Vallance and Linda Sellar in the Dunfermline Building Society ... Glasgow ...
>
> After pulling Helen by the hair, he forced her to the floor and put a knife to her neck.

Then he pushed both women into a strongroom and robbed them of £500.

... Defence counsel William Taylor said his client had robbed two building societies and a Chinese restaurant in Belfast with an unloaded rifle, also in August last year.

He gave himself up to police in Northern Ireland and confessed to all the offences in the hope that he could get psychiatric help in prison.[112]

In 1985 near Edinburgh two soldiers and a ex-major were shot dead and the army payroll they were carrying was stolen. The killings were professional and brutal and some papers speculated that the IRA must be responsible, until another soldier was charged, tried and sentenced:

A Royal Scots soldier was yesterday found guilty of the Army payroll killings and jailed for life, with a recommendation that he serve at least 30 years.

... The jury at the High Court in Edinburgh, took 90 minutes to reach a unanimous verdict. Corporal Andrew Walker, aged 31, was found guilty of shooting a retired army major and two serving soldiers on January 17, and robbing them of £19,000.

Lord Grieve, the judge, described the killings as 'brutal, callous and calculated'. The crime would bring revulsion to all right-thinking people, he said. Walker had shown himself to be unworthy to be a member of his 'famous and distinguished' regiment.

... Walker's weapon was a Sterling sub-machine-gun which he had signed out of the armoury using his position as an arms instructor.

... Walker's record as a regular soldier was first class. He had three tours of duty in Northern Ireland, on one of which he was mentioned in dispatches.[113]

In 1992, ex-para John Calton was jailed for 25 years for leading a 'terror gang' who stole £96,000 by holding families hostage:

He remained emotionless as Judge Peter Greenwood called him 'evil and wicked' and added: 'Your vile cruelty showed no mercy. You can expect none from me.'

The jury at Chelmsford Crown Court had heard a story that could have come from the BBC TV series Civvies.

Calton, who had served with the 1st Battalion Parachute Regiment, found no legal place in the outside world for his death-or-glory skills.

He had taken part in undercover missions in Northern Ireland, and an officer wrote in a chilling report on him: 'This man works very hard, but he has no regard for human life ...'

... In August last year, two masked men burst into Mr Andrews's [Tesco store boss] home ... and told him his family would be killed if he refused to co-operate.

His teenage sons were threatened with castration, and his wife believed she was about to be raped.

Mrs Andrews and the boys were taken to a remote wood, and Mr Andrews was ordered to go to work as usual ... and hand over £55,000 takings at the end of the day.[114]

Some veterans, looking for work and adventure, became mercenaries and fought for dubious regimes and causes in various parts of the world. Others hired out their killing skills at home. In 1987, ex-soldier Patrick Timlin was convicted for carrying out assassinations:

A former soldier called the 'cut-price killer' because of his willingness to shoot people was convicted yesterday of a murder plot against leading Sikh moderates in Britain.

... Timlin, of Lillington, Warwickshire, was paid just £6,000 to carry out two shootings in London. He killed one Sikh moderate – Mr Tarsem Toor, aged 55 – and partially blinded the second – Mr Singtar Singh Sandhu, aged 48 – by shooting them in the head with a sawn-off shotgun.[115]

In February 1988, police arrested some of West Ham United's violent fans called the Inter-City Firm. One of them had boasted on American TV that they were keeping up a British tradition of fighting wars and would have been heroes in the Falklands; 'Speaking on the video, which was shown to the court [he] said he felt "like Rambo" when he went to matches. "If we were doing all this in the Falklands they would love it. It's part of our heritage. The British have always been fighting wars"..."[116] Two months later an ex-para was on trial accused of leading a gang of Leeds United fans, known as Para's Army. Undercover police who had infiltrated the group stated, 'the men met in three Leeds city pubs and discussed football violence involving the police, black people and opposing fans.'[117] At the end of the trial, ex-para David Brown was jailed for four years. He was said to be the ringleader of Para's Army and had organised the attacks on opposing fans with military precision:

> The court was told that Brown, a former Salvation Army bandsman, experienced violent fantasies and was probably suffering 'post traumatic stress disorder' – known as battle shock during the last war – as a result of acting as a 2nd Bn Parachute Regiment medical orderly at Goose Green and Bluff Cove during the Falklands campaign.[118]

The attacks launched on civilians by serving and ex-soldiers are often directed against women or gays. In 1977, serving soldiers Dale Martin and Anthony Bottril were jailed for killing two homosexual men:

> Two Coldstream Guardsmen who allowed themselves to be 'picked up' in a pub frequented by homosexuals intending to rob their victim finished up with a blood bath in which two men were stabbed to death, an Old Bailey jury was told yesterday.
>
> One of the slaughtered men was the Lord Mayor's valet, Dennis Chalke (39), and the other John Fore (48), tour operator. Their bodies were found in a blood-spattered flat ...
>
> ... Prosecuting counsel told the jury that both guardsmen left their barracks on Saturday, May 21, to go on weekend leave and they called at a military shop in Eton where Martin bought a Bowie knife and Bottril a throwing knife.
>
> They then went to London and in the evening went to the 'Golden Lion', Dean-St., Soho, a pub said to be frequented by homosexuals.
>
> They struck up a conversation with Mr Fore who bought them drinks and took them back to the ... flat where Mr Chalke was staying the weekend.
>
> "The guardsmen allowed themselves to be invited to the flat, probably for homosexual purposes, and they went with the intention of robbing, each

armed with a knife," said counsel.

When the bodies were found both had numerous wounds to their backs and chests and Mr Fore's jugular vein had been slit.[119]

In 1996, an ex-soldier was jailed for life for trying to kill a man who had picked him up in a bar:

George Rees, from Manchester, who suffered homosexual rape and abuse during his career in the Blues and Royals Cavalry Regiment, taunted Tony Grundy about his sexual tastes and then stabbed him three times with a large kitchen knife.

When police arrested him he told them he had also wanted to kill the former East Enders actor and gay activist Michael Cashman for his campaign to end the controversial ban on homosexuals in the armed forces.

He said that during his time in the army he was raped by a male colleague and frequently bullied, tortured and abused.

Passing sentence, judge Richard Hawkins, QC, said the motive for his attack had been a combination of 'homophobia and a desire to steal'.[120]

In 1991, Gerard Lamb, an ex-para, was jailed for five years at the Old Bailey for a bayonet attack on his ex-girlfriend and her lover as they lay in bed:

Gerard Lamb, aged 31, was convicted of causing grievous bodily harm, with intent, to actress Patricia Minskoff, 23, and Warren McCormack, 24.

The court was told how Mr Lamb stabbed the couple repeatedly. ...

Police, alerted by a lodger, arrived to find Miss Minskoff bleeding heavily.[121]

In 1997, the *Express* told about the 'Mystery of the soldier who killed just for fun':

Random killer Derek Christian was last night locked away along with the reason why he murdered a great-grandmother in a quiet country lane.

After the ex-soldier and father of three was jailed for life, the detective who caught him said: 'We will probably never know the answer.'

Farmer's wife Margaret Wilson, 66, became Christian's victim as she strolled in broad daylight. He leapt from his car and slashed her throat from ear to ear in what psychologists called a 'recreational killing'.

... Det Chief Insp Martin Midgley said: 'This was a random, motiveless killing. Usually, there is some connection between a killer and victim. We

Wife killer is jailed for life

By TOM MERRIN

A SCOTS former soldier was yesterday jailed for life for murdering his ex-wife.

Bill Duncan, 54, stabbed her last November with a combat knife.

Winchester Crown Court was told Martina, 44, divorced her husband of 20 years when she inherited £500,000.

He had stalked Tina for 10 days before attacking her yards from their former marital home in Poole, Dorset.

Despite three operations and a massive blood transfusion, the mother of two died three days later.

Meanwhile, Duncan fled north and tried to give himself up to police in Edinburgh. But the court heard he was turned away.

Duncan then phoned Dorset police to repeat his confession and he was eventually arrested by red-faced Edinburgh cops at his mum's home in Clermiston.

DAILY RECORD 23/6/92

Three years for double mugger

AN ex-soldier carried out a brutal mugging while on bail for a similar attack.

And yesterday 23-year-old William Wood was jailed for three years.

Inverness Sheriff Court heard Wood had been thrown out of the Black Watch for being a drug addict.

In November he was approached in an Inverness pub by a man wanting to buy cannabis.

Victim

Wood pretended he could help, found out how much he wanted, then took him outside and punched and kicked him senseless. His victim had severe bruising.

Wood was arrested and released on bail.

But in February he hit another ... the head ... whi...

A smashing place to sleep

A FORMER soldier smashed a shop window to get a place to sleep.

And yesterday James Stirling, 35, of Bonnybridge, was fined £400 at Stirling Sheriff Court and ordered to pay £607 to replace the window.

Soldiers used terror tactics for robberies

THREE soldiers used terrorist tactics they witnessed in Northern Ireland to carry out a violent robbery campaign, an Old Bailey jury heard yester...

... yres, aged 19, Ian ..., and Zenon Brown ... imitation handguns ... camouflage jackets ...as. They raided a ... held two motor... in Sevenoaks, ... a post office

... to the streets ... methods which ...ose they had been ...Northern Ireland," ...ompus, prosecuting. ... court heard the men ...raumatised in Ulster ...ve been exhibiting ...c stress syndrome. ... arrested after rob... office in Enfield,

...Buckhurst Hill, ... of Bletchley, ...e, and Mr ...s address as ... pleaded guilty ...y to rob and posses... imitation firearm.

Recorder Penry-Davey, remanded them in custody pre-sentencing reports.

FR... BI... BR... SCOTS SOLDIER

By DAVID LOVE

A SOLDIER who survived an IRA fire attack in Northern Ireland was fined £400 yesterday for attempted fraud.

Royal Scot Lance-Corporal Stephen Mathie was under stress before going on the tour, Inverness Sheriff Court heard.

And he used a stolen bank pass-book to try to

Derek defeats the red tape

FORMER commando Derek McAdam has just won the battle of his life ... over red tape.

But it has taken almost 20 years to prove that action in Northern Ireland had mentally affected the Dublin-born Royal Marine.

Now, at last, 60-year-old Derek has been awarded a lump sum of £25,000 and a pension of almost £200 a week.

Derek, from Boat of Garten, Inverness-shire, joined the Marines in 1956 and saw service overseas.

But it was in the early 1970s when he was posted to Northern Ireland that things started to go wrong.

Derek said: "I was a weapons instructor and I was training commandos to shoot my countrymen.

"This split in loyalties began to make me very depressed and I was sent to a military psychiatric hospital."

He was medically discharged but the MoD and the then DHSS refused to accept his depression had been caused by his service in Ireland.

His battle against bureaucracy only ended a few weeks ago when Mr K. N. Murray, who had originally treated Derek, agreed to assess him for another appeal to the Pension Appeal Tribunal.

Derek said: "It was the breakthrough in the fight to get justice."

still don't know what his motive was and we probably never will.'[122]

In 1996, a violent tragedy happened on the Goose Green army estate in Aldershot as 'A Paratrooper butchered his wife and her best pal – then leapt to his death from a car park':

Darran Mallia is thought to have been distraught over the break-up of his marriage five weeks ago.

Police found his wife Alexia and her best pal Allison Williams stabbed to death at the Mallias' Army married quarters.

Both were still in their night clothes. A kitchen knife was found lying nearby.

Allison, 34, had moved in with Alexia, 27, after Darran had left.

Just minutes before the bodies were found, Darran had been seen launching himself off a multi-storey car park.

A witness said he dived with his hands behind his back and splattered onto the ground below.

... A fellow Para said: 'All Paras are wild but Taff was known as a bit of a nutter. He had tattoos all over him and liked to walk around with his shirt off.

'He had just come back from the Purple Star exercise in the US, he'd been in Ireland recently and was going to Ireland again.

'The pressure of Ireland and the fact that his relationship was up the spout must have been too much.'[123]

Unsurprisingly, the greatest concentrations of serving soldiers' involvement in violence and crime takes place in or around garrison areas, often after the return of units from tours of duty in Northern Ireland. In 1997, the *Sunday Times* Insight Team investigated this:

The number of convictions in civilian courts – the most reliable independent indicator of serious army crime, according to legal experts – shows that offences involving drugs and violence committed by soldiers have increased dramatically. In 1995, the latest year for which figures are available, there were 289 convictions. Of these, there were 38 convictions for drugs offences – an increase of 80% on the previous year. Figures released this weekend by the office of the judge advocate general, Judge James Rant QC, reveal that the crime wave has hit all the big army garrisons in Britain.

Bulford in Wiltshire, headquarters of the army's Third Division, has the worst record. In six years to the end of 1996, local courts-martial heard 77 cases involving serious crimes of violence and drugs, Aldershot, headquarters of the Parachute Regiment, had 73 courts-martial cases; Catterick, an infantry training garrison, logged 71. David Howell, a former military prosecutor, said the number of courts martial in Aldershot reflected the type of soldier in the Parachute Regiment.

'If you train these people to the peak of fitness and tell them how to attack an enemy and then they take a lot of drink, little disagreements are bound to lead to an incident,' he said.[124]

The cases I have cited in this chapter are only a few representative examples, the tip of the iceberg. In the absence of official statistics detailing the number of ex-soldiers in British prisons, some of the jailed veterans have tried to find out the figures for themselves. Based on replies to ads placed in the prisoners' paper *Inside Time* and on head-counts taken inside prisons, they believe that between 4 and 7 per cent of prisoners are ex-squaddies. With the prison population in England and Wales totalling over 63,000 in early 1998, this suggests that several thousand prisoners are ex-soldiers (Scottish prisons probably have a similar proportion). Certainly, over the past three decades thousands of Northern Ireland veterans have served time in British jails and there are many hundreds still in the prison system:

Dr Morgan O'Connell, an ex-armed forces consultant psychiatrist, says a separate prison should be established to deal with the needs of increasing numbers of former servicemen now behind bars.

Dr O'Connell, who was attached to the Royal Navy and was with the Forces in the Falklands war, claims there are a disproportionate number of ex-servicemen in the prison system suffering from mental disorders like PTSD.

He recently set up a PTSD management programme at Holy Cross Hospital in Haslemere, Surrey, and was struck by the number of ex-servicemen attending fresh from prison.

Dr O'Connell says there needs to be a special therapeutic community established to deal with the problems of the ex-servicemen.

'I'm not trying to say that they should not be in prison but that their misbehaviour reflects a traumatic experience they endured while serving their country and that condition needs to be examined.'

PTSD is a syndrome arising out of an unusual experience – the experience that created the condition is trapped in the victim's memory and can be triggered at any time.

When the event involves extreme violence, failure to treat the condition means that the victim is in effect 'a walking time-bomb' waiting to go off at any time.[125]

As a consequence of not receiving any help for their rehabilitation back into Civvie Street, or treatment for conditions like PTSD, many of these ex-soldiers found themselves without a job, homeless and often drinking to excess and/or taking drugs. A course that frequently led to trouble, violence and jail. Since 1969, probably more deaths and injuries have been inflicted on the civilian population in Britain by our returning soldiers than by IRA bombings. Like the USA after Vietnam, the war has come home.

Hidden Wounds

In the USA, the Vietnam veterans campaigned about PTSD and other problems to do with their resettlement back into civilian life. *The Viet-Vet Survival Guide* starts its section on Psychological Readjustment like this:

Most people think the Vietnam war was over in 1975. A lot of Viet Vets know they're wrong. For hundreds of thousands of vets – and their loved ones – the psychological effects of the war are a part of everyday life. Most of these vets suffer from Post-Traumatic Stress Disorder (PTSD). Some have other war-related psychological problems or a war-related dependence on drugs or alcohol.

... For most Viet Vets, the adjustment back to civilian life posed few or no major problems. But for others – perhaps as many as 40% of vets who served in Vietnam – things haven't gone well. In fact, sometimes things seem to be getting progressively worse. These and other complaints are often heard:

'I can't keep a job.'

'I have no skills or training that will get me a decent job.'

'I feel my life is going nowhere.'

'I can't stay in a relationship. I've been married and divorced [once or several times] and the same thing keeps happening over and over again – I go so far and that's it.'

'I just can't get close to anybody. I don't trust anybody.'

'Sometimes I have nightmares about the 'Nam or I wake up in a cold sweat, trembling.'

'I'm always tense, wired for something to happen, can't relax.'

'I thought when I left Vietnam I left all that behind me, but things keep coming back – memories, thoughts, feelings, for no apparent reason.'

'I feel so dead [or empty] inside, just numb to people and things that happen.'

'I started drinking [or taking drugs] over there and now I've started again.'

'I just don't fit in anywhere in society.'

'I look around, and I seem to be the only one who is having these emotional problems.'

'During certain times of the year I just seem to lose it, and that's not normal.'

'I feel so alone.'

'I don't know what's happening to me.'

'At times I think I must be going crazy.'

'How can something that happened ten, fifteen, twenty years ago still be influencing my life.'

... The feelings expressed in the quotations just given can be a normal reaction to an abnormal situation, such as war. But when the normal healing process of adjusting to terrible experiences becomes disrupted, a normal stress reaction can worsen, becoming a 'stress disorder'.[126]

The Vietnam veterans struggled to get the US government to recognise these problems officially and to get the American people to come to terms with these occurrences. The veterans had to show courage and tenacity in taking their message to the American people, because there were many who were hostile, or who did not want to hear:

There is ... considerable rage, much of it beneath the surface, towards
Vietnam veterans. They are resented both for not winning the war and
thereby being agents of humiliation, and also for the 'dirty' things they have
done. Moreover, they are deeply feared by a society that sense their potential
violence and is all too quick to label them as 'drug addicts' or 'killers' – and
this kind of fear can be quickly converted into rage.

Finally, there are large elements of American society enraged at – because
deeply threatened by – the antiwar veterans' transformation. For that
transformation depends directly upon exposing the filth beneath the
warrior's claim to purity of mission, upon subverting much that is
fundamental to American warrior mythology. Americans profoundly
involved with that mythology may experience considerable rage towards
these bearers of bad news, whom they may then blame for the news itself –
for the decline of the old virtues. Underneath that rage are the profound
doubts of everyone, even those who would most like to remain true believers
in all aspects of American glory.[127]

After years of campaigning the Vietnam veterans began to win over public support. Roderick Ørner, the District Clinical Psychologist for Lincoln, contrasted the treatment of Vietnam veterans with British Falklands war veterans. In an article in the *Psychologist*, he told how, less than five years after the USA's withdrawal from Vietnam, a conference was convened to 'review the status and predicament of the veterans of United States military engagement in South East Asia':

Speakers from the fields of law, political science, philosophy, sociology,
economics, psychology and psychiatry lent credibility to the campaigns of
veterans' groups. Thirteen years after the Falklands War it is doubtful if
enough data have been gathered about our veterans group to even consider

arranging a similar conference in the United Kingdom. Even less so for Northern Ireland veterans or veterans of the Gulf War.

All of this is entirely consistent with the impression left by recent commemorations of the end of World War Two. The welfare and welfare rights of British war veterans have so far not attained high public priority. At this moment of reckoning, it is clear that those who should have represented the interests of British ex-service personnel returning from war and their families, leave a shameful record. This may be a consequence of a conspiracy of silence and sanitation in relation to truths about wars and their aftermath.[128]

An idea of the extent of the plight of ex-soldiers in Britain today can be gleaned from a research study, *Falling Out*, produced by CRISIS in 1994. The study looked at homeless ex-service people in London and stated among its main conclusions:

   • Ex-service homeless people are disproportionately represented amongst single homeless people – around one quarter of all single homeless people have served in the forces.

   • Ex-service homeless people are even more disadvantaged than other homeless people – they are on average older, more likely to sleep rough and have been homeless for longer.

   • Many ex-service homeless people have problems other than a lack of a home and are likely to need resettlement support.

   • Only a minority of ex-service homeless people received help with housing and other problems when they left the services and many were dissatisfied with the help they did receive.[129]

The survey was carried out among ex-service people staying in hostels and attending day centres in central London. 67 per cent of the respondents had served in the army, 29 per cent had been in alcohol dependence units, 41 per cent had spent time in prison. Many complained about the lack of help they received when they left the services: 'You see the Resettlement Officer about six months before you leave. He sent me for one job interview and the people there weren't interested when I got there. ... Most people go straight into the Army from school.

They should prepare them for Civvy Street.'[130] 29 per cent of ex-service people interviewed said they were suffering from nerves, depression and stress; 23 per cent had been treated in psychiatric units. Some said their service life had been psychologically damaging; 'I feel that being in the Army turned my brain a bit. I was in two hostile areas. I still have nightmares now. I wake up screaming. ... They should do more for people.'[131]

In Britain, anyone raising the issue of Northern Ireland veterans suffering from psychological problems after their tours of duty can expect to face hostility from the military establishment. In 1992, Lynda La Plante's TV drama *Civvies* was broadcast. La Plante wrote *Civvies* after some ex-paras did some building work in her home and told her about themselves. The series was about the violent lives of ex-paras:

> Karl Francis, the director, believes that it reflects a much bigger real life
> story which has yet to be told.
>
> As a self-styled radical film maker, Francis admits to finding the theme of
> *Civvies* a challenge: 'Instead of looking at the hearts and minds of the
> communities the soldiers have tried to conquer, it looked at the minds of the
> soldiers themselves – trying to conquer their own demons and live with them
> afterwards.
>
> 'I've got cousins and friends who've been in the army,' he says. 'I've heard
> how they try and deal with the stress – their wives have told me. I've met the
> soldiers who ended up pill-poppers and drug addicts. I've listened to the
> awful stories of their dreams.
>
> 'People respond to soldiering in different ways. Being a soldier doesn't
> make you a good or a bad person. The lads in *Civvies* came out of the army
> still fighting, they were all wounded emotionally, they wanted healing.'
>
> He does not lean towards sentimentality: 'They were screwed up. And
> yes, they were victims. But they dished it out as well, and if you deliver hell,
> sometimes it comes round on you and you have to live with it.'[132]

Lynda La Plante made friends with the group of ex-paras she had met and based her drama *Civvies* on. She tried to help them settle back into civilian life; 'But, by the time the show was broadcast, every single one of the soldiers she'd met and found jobs for was in prison. ... She said, "The show was an angry plea to the Government to do something about PTSD.""[133] There was no doubt that *Civvies* was La Plante's most difficult and controversial series. It was described as 'offensive' by the Defence Ministry, and as 'inaccurate, belittling and will demoralise the troops' by the Parachute Regiment. Later Lynda La Plante commented; '*Civvies* is an open wound. ... Nothing in *Civvies* hadn't happened. It wasn't a fictional drama. It was fact, all of it. Yet I was vilified and abused by everybody. The shoals of letters I still get; "That was my brother, that was my father, that was my uncle, that was my husband.""[134]

Inside the military, some concerned doctors in the medical corps attempted to set up programmes to prevent PTSD and centres to deal with it when it occurs. But their efforts foundered on the indifference shown by their superiors:

Major Jeffrey McPherson, the senior lecturer in psychiatry at Woolwich Military Hospital, was close to the gods in Army psychiatry. Along with Surgeon Commander Morgan O'Connell of the Navy, he recognised the need for proper provision for PTSD. In 1987 he formed the first PTSD group at Woolwich without any policy or direct financial support from the Army medical hierarchy. His intention was to establish the Army's first clinic...

McPherson recalls: 'It was really a one-man-and-a-dog affair. We received no encouragement, and had to fit it in where we could, which, at its height, amounted to half a day a week. However, the few we were able to treat – about 70 in all – responded well; we had a high success rate in getting rid of symptoms; but it was poor as far as going back and serving. Most of the guys were discharged out of the service.'

He continued to press the Directorate for a proper PTSD programme and educational and preventive courses during training. 'They gave it a lot of lip service but in the end simply posted me to Germany, which is the Army's way of saying "Give up."' Which is what he did. Both he and his most experienced behavioural therapist, John Rose, resigned from the Army in despair.[135]

After officially recognising that some Vietnam veterans were suffering rehabilitation problems, the US government authorised the setting up of a testing programme for PTSD and provided treatment for those found to be suffering from this disorder. In 1979, the American Congress sanctioned the setting up of Veteran Centres, and over the next five years nearly two hundred were established across the United States. The centres had an informal atmosphere and many of the staff were Vietnam era veterans:

> Once in a Vet Centre – surrounded by other vets, and benefiting from counselling – the vet often begins to unburden himself. He talks about the war with others who understand, and who accept what he says without being frightened and without condemning him for his statements. In many cases, the vet begins to feel no longer alone or isolated. He realises he's not crazy, that his problems can be worked out, and that he need no longer run from these problems.[136]

During a visit to a Veteran Centre in Detroit, I showed the staff the letter I had received from Northern Ireland veteran Jimmy Johnson. They immediately said; 'This is a cry for help, just like the ones we get all the time from Vietnam vets.' In Frankland Prison Johnson became acutely aware of how his condition had affected others. In *Their Country's Reward* he expressed his regrets and sorrow to his wife and children and the families of his victims: 'To my wife Maureen, my son Jimmy and my daughter Andrea. To the families of Mr Keith Culmner and Mr Robin Harwood. I'm sorry, I'm sorry – I did not know!' Jimmy also had this message for the authorities in Britain:

> I accuse the British Government and the Ministry of Defence of a complete betrayal of its own soldiers and their families. They are keeping silent and trying to hide the fact that a large majority of serving and ex-serving soldiers are suffering from Post Traumatic Stress Disorder. Many of these men have served in Northern Ireland. ...
>
> The Government are saying, 'There is no quick-fix to this war.' But there are no de-sensitisation programmes either to help and treat the returning soldiers, who, after many months of being under intense stress and suffering traumatic experiences are being left to cope with this disorder by themselves. With the MoD's uncaring attitude and with ignoring the truth that PTSD is

affecting their soldiers, they are inflicting more damage to their own men –
more than any terrorist organisation could ever hope to achieve.[137]

Compared to Vietnam, the level of conflict in Northern Ireland was clearly not on the same scale. But, it has lasted for nearly three decades and much of the
day-to-day violence – squaddies versus locals – went unreported in the media.
British soldiers were indoctrinated for the occupation of nationalist areas and
trained to use violence to assert their presence and resolve any disputes in their
favour. Consequently, some soldiers were affected by their military experiences,
liable to react to stress in the only way they know – violently – by lashing out at
those nearest them. Many of these men are suffering from the hidden wound of
conflict – PTSD.

John Mackenzie is the solicitor who won an out of court settlement of
£100,000 from the MoD for ex-Scots Guardsman Alex Findlay. Mackenzie, who
spent five years researching PTSD and its effects on veterans, said about
the MoD:

> They just don't care. The MoD is interested in servicemen so long as
> they remain fit and compliant, but as soon as they cease to fit that mould then
> the comfortable image it tries to portray of caring, family-style units,
> particularly regiments, goes out of the window. It's just a marketing ploy that
> has no basis in reality. This [PTSD] is a terrifying, horrifying, appalling
> disorder, ... now I'm afraid that it's too late for a lot of these guys. They are
> ruined humans and they want an acknowledgement of their condition and
> their suffering.[138]

During the peace process in Northern Ireland, both republicans and loyalists have made it clear that any settlement to the conflict cannot be concluded till
all their prisoners are freed. They regard their prisoners as prisoners of the war
and declare they would not be in jail but for the political situation that existed in
Northern Ireland. A considerable number of ex-soldiers who once served in Her
Majesty's Armed Forces in Ireland have subsequently served time in Her
Majesty's Prisons. They have been abandoned by their military and political leaders and their cries for help are ignored. These are Britain's forgotten prisoners of
the war, but there is no one to take their part or campaign on their behalf and there

Jimmy Johnson's letter to the author ▶

18/5/90

627710. J.Johnson.
A.Wing.
H.M.Prison Frankland
Brasside
Durham.
DH15YD.

Sir.

Having just read your recent book, "Last Night Another Soldier."
I found it most interesting and realistic.
I also realised that you must have been in touch with many other
troops who have served in N. Ireland.
I myself have served in the army for ten years, 14 months in Aden.
(1965-1966) and also a 4 month and a 12 month tour of duty in N.-
Ireland. I was also mentioned in despatches whilst serving in
N.Ireland.
Immediately upon my 12 months tour in Ireland I bought myself
out of the army, For family reasons.
Upon returning to civilian life I found that I could not settle
in or indeed adjust in any way.
Although I had the offer of several steady and permanent jobs
I simply could not cope.
My marriage which had been under great strain whilst I was in Ireland
now fell apart.
After that it was all down hill and within a mere four months of
leaving the army, and my chosen career. I found myself in prison
with a long sentence, hence the address.
Once in prison I was surprised to find quite a number of ex- soldiers
and N.Ireland veterans as fellow inmates.
A much higher percentage I would suspect than average for any other
profession.
This as set me to thinking of the American experience in Viet-Nam
and the major adjustment problems their veterans have had upon
their return also the more recent but similar problems the Russians
have experienced with their vets from Afghanistan.
Now it really would be too much to believe that the British Soldier
had come unscathed through 20 years of stress and trauma,
professional and efficient though he undoubtably is.
I also believe that the M.O.D. people, Doctors, Psycholagists etc,
have been monitoring the situation very carefully ever since 1970.
about twice as long as Viet Nam.
now the Americans have made no secret of their findings and
problems nor indeed have the Russians.
But from us the British there is a total deafening silence.
Consequently I would greatly appreciate any comment or opinion
you might have on this whole aspect of what might best be
described as post N. Ireland Trauma.
I would also be very grateful for any material, (if it exists)
that might be avialable from any source whatsoever.

Hoping that you will find this letter thought provoking
and that it will meet with your favourable consideration,
thank you.

Yours Faithfully.

J. Johnson

By the QUEEN'S Order the name of

23974251 CPL J JOHNSON - R T R -

was published in the London Gazette on

3 DECEMBER 1972

as mentioned in a Despatch for distinguished service.
I am charged to record
Her Majesty's high appreciation.

Carrington

Secretary of State for Defence

LAWYERS TO APPEAL OVER DOUBLE KILLER 'TRAUMATISED' BY ULSTER'S VIOLENCE

Legal aid for the ex-soldier who claims he murdered in 'flashback'

EXCLUSIVE by SEAN RAYMENT
Defence Correspondent

A DOUBLE killer has won legal aid to appeal against his conviction after claiming he was driven to murder by mental stress.

James Johnson blames the killings on the violence he experienced as a soldier on the streets of Northern Ireland.

Now his lawyers have been granted thousands of pounds in legal aid for a test case appeal and Johnson could be released in months. Yet only last year he was considered such a danger to society that Home Secretary Michael Howard ruled that, for him, life should mean life.

Central to the appeal is that 49-year-old Johnson was suffering from post-traumatic stress disorder — a condition unknown when he murdered in 1974 and 1985. The former Royal Tank Regiment corporal claims his PTSD stems from two experiences in Ulster. In one, he recovered the body of a woman killed in a terrorist explosion. The other was a street riot during which he says he battered a civilian almost to death. Both incidents, he told psychiatrists, left him traumatised.

Within weeks of leaving the Army, father of two Johnson murdered a security guard from whom he stole just £60. In an interview with a psychiatrist, Johnson remembers being offered a lift by the guard.

He says: 'I've a vague recollection of kids playing on the side of the road. All I remember is a crash on the side of the van. I think kids had thrown something at it. The next thing I remember is running. I was carrying Keith (his victim). I dragged him down. I battered him

Ex-soldier claims Ulster stress led him to kill twice

By Paul Donovan

JAMES JOHNSON sits alone in his cell in Frankland Prison, Co Durham, with only his nightmares for company. He is approaching the half-way point in a 30-year sentence for murder.

Johnson believes the two unprovoked murders he committed are attributable to the stress he suffered while a young soldier in Northern Ireland. He believes that

Johnson in Army days

Chilling diary of death is bid for medical aid

BRUTAL double killer Jimmy Johnson has issued a desperate Christmas plea for help from his prison cell.

The former East Lancashire army-hero-turned-murderer has written a chilling diary of death in a bid to get help from a pioneering doctor.

Johnson is serving life after battering Blackburn bachelor Robert Harwood, in 1986.

He was on parole after serving part of another life sentence for murdering a Teesside security officer.

Now, Johnson wants to bring his case to the attention of Dr Roderick Orner — a specialist in Post Traumatic Stress Disorder.

PTSA, thought to affect Vietnam and other war veterans, is a delayed shock which is thought to lead to extreme personality disorders.

By SHARON DALE

Johnson believes the horrors and hatred he experienced as a soldier in Northern Ireland left him scarred for life.

are hundreds, perhaps thousands, of them still serving time in British jails.

Northern Ireland veterans, like the men of the First World War and the GIs after Vietnam, are not looking for pity. They do think, however, that they can ask for our understanding. They also seek our help to publicise their predicament and put pressure on the authorities to publicly acknowledge that many ex-soldiers, on their return from tours of duty in Northern Ireland, have had experiences that parallel those of the Vietnam veterans.

Like in the USA after Vietnam, the key is for the British authorities to officially recognise that many British soldiers who served in Northern Ireland have ended up in Civvy Street facing psychological and/or other rehabilitation problems. Publicity should then be given to the issue, to explain it and gain public awareness, understanding and support. Testing and treatment can then be set in motion for those ex-soldiers who are suffering from post-traumatic stress disorder. For serving soldiers there needs to be de-briefings after active service and a comprehensive re-training programme to help veterans settle back into civilian life. Writing from his prison cell, Jimmy Johnson concluded his book, *Their Country's Reward*, with these lines:

'As an ex-soldier, having served tours of duty in Northern Ireland, it took eighteen years before someone enlightened me that I had been suffering from PTSD. Now that I know about this disorder I shall not keep quiet about it. I shall do my utmost to expose the Government and the MoD's callous indifference to the fighting men, who are still unknowingly suffering from this disorder because of active service seen in Northern Ireland.

If the Government needs to commit their soldiers into a war of unknown and faceless enemies, then, they should help their soldiers and not betray them – which the Government and the MoD, with their conspiracy to keep silent, are doing. The MoD must ensure that their stressed and traumatised soldiers have a psychological return ticket, back to a normal life, and are not cast aside like a piece of discarded equipment.

The soldiers and ex-soldiers who have served in Northern Ireland

have to be switched off! The families of these men know that I am right. They know that they did not get their true husbands or sons back from these "tours of duty" in Northern Ireland'.

[1] *Panorama*, BBC1 TV, 26th April 1976.

[2] *Fire Power*, by Chris Dempster and Dave Tomkins, Corgi 1978.

[3] *Ibid*.

[4] *Observer*, 30th July 1995.

[5] *Ibid*.

[6] *Daily Mirror*, 1st Oct. 1980.

[7] *Ibid*.

[8] *Sun*, 21st July 1990.

[9] *Daily Mail*, 21st July 1991.

[10] *Observer Magazine*, 10th June 1990, detailed five page article by Peter Nasmyth.

[11] *Ibid*.

[12] *Ibid*.

[13] *Ibid*.

[14] *Henry IV, Part One*, by William Shakespeare, Act 2, Scene 3.

[15] *American Heritage*, May/June 1990, article on shell shock by Roger J Spiller.

[16] *The Rambling Soldier*, edited by Roy Palmer, Penguin Books 1977.

[17] *War Machine – The Rationalisation of Slaughter in the Modern Age*, by Daniel Pick, Yale University Press 1993.

[18] *Sassoon's Long Journey*, edited by Paul Fussell, Faber and Faber 1983.

[19] *War Machine – The Rationalisation of Slaughter in the Modern Age*, by Daniel Pick, Yale University Press 1993.

[20] See *Shot at Dawn*, by Julian Putkowski and Julian Sykes, Wharncliffe Publishing Ltd 1989.

[21] *War Machine – The Rationalisation of Slaughter in the Modern Age*, by Daniel Pick, Yale University Press 1993.

[22] *Monthly News Sheet*, Women's International League, Oct. 1920.

[23] *Ibid*.

[24] *Boldness Be My Friend*, by Richard Pape.

[25] *Catch-22*, by Joseph Heller, Jonathan Cape Edition 1962, Corgi Edition 1964.

[26] *Guardian*, 19th July 1995, obituary of Richard Pape by Dan van der Vat.

[27] *Battle for the Mind*, by William Sargant, Pan Books Ltd. 1959.

[28] *Home From the War – Vietnam Veterans neither Victims or Executioners*, by Robert Jay Lifton, Beacon Press Boston 1992.

[29] From author David Morrell's introduction to *First Blood*, Headline Feature 1992.

[30] *Home From the War – Vietnam Veterans neither Victims or Executioners*, by Robert Jay Lifton, Beacon Press Boston 1992.

[31] *The Viet Vet Survival Guide*, by Craig Kubey, David F Addlestone, Richard E O'Dell, Keith D Snyder, Barton F Stichman and Vietnam Veterans of America, Ballantine Books, New York 1985.

[32] *Home From the War – Vietnam Veterans neither Victims or Executioners*, by Robert Jay Lifton, Beacon Press Boston 1992.

[33] *Ibid.*

[34] *Ibid.*

[35] *The Murders of the Black Museum 1870-1970*, by Gordon Honeycombe, Bloomsbury Books 1992.

[36] *Ibid.*

[37] *The Ambiguities of Power – British Foreign Policy Since 1945*, by Mark Curtis, Zed Books 1995.

[38] Rex Flowers, who served with the Lincolnshire Regiment, told in *Six Campaigns – National Servicemen at War 1948-1960*, edited by Adrian Walker, Leo Cooper 1993.

[39] *The Malayan Emergency: The Commonwealth's War 1948-1966*, by Robert Jackson, Routledge 1991.

[40] *Guardian*, 2nd Feb. 1993.

[41] *More Murders of the Black Museum 1835-1985*, by Gordon Honeycombe, Arrow Books 1994.

[42] *Ibid.*

[43] Ron Hawkes, who served with the Royal Irish Fusiliers, told in *Six Campaigns – National Servicemen at War 1948-1960*, edited by Adrian Walker, Leo Cooper 1993.

[44] *More Murders of the Black Museum 1835-1985*, by Gordon Honeycombe, Arrow Books 1994.

[45] *The Black Panther Story*, by Steven Valentine, New English Library 1976.

[46] *Daily Mail*, 13th Aug. 1966.

[47] *The Dirty War*, by Martin Dillon, Hutchinson 1988.

[48] *Sunday Mail* [Scotland], 17th Dec. 1978; also the editions of the paper on 26th April, 3rd May, 10th May and 17th May 1981.

[49] *Monthly Review*, Nov. 1970.

[50] *City Limits*, 16–22 July 1982.

[51] *Ibid.*

[52] *Guardian*, 12th Nov. 1993, by Stephen Boulton and Christian Jennings of *World in Action*.

[53] *Morning Star*, 14th Feb. 1989.

[54] *Ibid.*

[55] *Mail on Sunday Magazine*, 15th Jan. 1995, article on soldiers and PTSD by Jean Rafferty.

[56] *Ibid.*

[57] *Ibid.*

[58] *Observer*, 27th Feb. 1994.

[59] *Daily Record*, 26th Feb. 1997.

[60] *Guardian*, 1st Nov. 1982.

[61] *Observer*, 30th Aug. 1992, article and interview by David Rose.

[62] *Ibid.*

[63] *Ibid.*

[64] *Daily Mirror*, front page, 26th February 1979.

[65] *Daily Mirror*, 26th February 1979.

[66] *Sunday Telegraph*, 7th April 1974.

[67] *Time Out*, no. 486, 10–16 Aug. 1979.

[68] *Observer Magazine*, 13th March 1994.

[69] Private Ken J. interviewed by Tony Parker, in *Soldier, Soldier*, Heinemann Ltd 1985.

[70] *The Viet Vet Survival Guide*, Ballantine Books, New York 1985.

[71] *Daily Record*, 13th May 1994.

[72] *Irish Post*, 18th Jan. 1992.

[73] *The British Media and Ireland*, article by Philip Elliot, Information on Ireland 1979.

[74] *Humo*, 10th and 17th Aug. 1989, ex-soldier Dave Roach interviewed by Jan Hertoghs.

[75] *Ibid.*

[76] *Daily Mail*, 11th Jan. 1990.

[77] *New Society*, Dec. 1972.

[78] *Soldier Magazine*, Feb. 1980.

[79] *Guardian*, 18th Jan. 1994.

[80] *New Statesman*, 16th Jan. 1976.

[81] *Spectator*, 25th Jan. 1992.

[82] *Sunday Telegraph*, 7th April 1974.

[83] *Evening News*, 26th Feb. 1979.

[84] *Horizon*, Feb. 1942.

[85] *All Bull: The National Servicemen*, edited by B S Johnson, Quartet Books Ltd. 1973.

[86] *Contact*, by A F N Clarke, Pan Books 1984.

[87] *Shoot To Kill – A soldier's journey through violence*, by Michael Asher, Penguin Books 1991.

[88] Jimmy Johnson's letter to the author from A Wing, HM Prison Frankland, 18th May 1990.

[89] 'Their Country's Reward', by Jimmy Johnson, unpublished.

[90] *Ibid.*

[91] *Ibid.*

[92] *Ibid.*

[93] *Trauma and Recovery – From Domestic Abuse to Political Terror*, by Judith Lewis Herman, Pandora 1994.

[94] *Daily Mail*, 9th April 1996, article by Sean Rayment.

[95] *Ibid.*

[96] 'Their Country's Reward', by Jimmy Johnson, unpublished.

[97] *Guardian*, 29th Oct. 1997.

[98] *Daily Record*, 5th May 1992.

[99] *Daily Mail*, 19th Aug. 1981.

[100] *Today*, 20th Oct. 1990.

[101] *Leicester Mercury*, 1st Feb. 1991.

[102] *Leicester Mercury*, 17th July 1993.

[103] *Evening News* [Cambridge], 21st Oct. 1997.

[104] *Guardian*, 18th Dec. 1993.

[105] *Daily Record*, 16th Feb. 1991.

[106] *Sun*, 11th Aug. 1994, article by Mike Ridley and John Kay.

[107] *Sun*, 13th Aug. 1994.

[108] *You*, the *Mail on Sunday* magazine, 23rd April 1989.

[109] *Guardian*, 21st Nov. 1994, article by Duncan Campbell and Kevin Rushby.

[110] *Daily Record*, 18th Aug. 1992.

[111] *Daily Record*, 23rd Jan. 1987.

[112] *Daily Record*, 17th Oct. 1985.

[113] *Times*, 18th May 1985.

[114] *Daily Mail*, 13th Nov. 1992.

[115] *Times*, 30th Oct. 1987.

[116] *Daily Telegraph*, 3rd Feb. 1988.

[117] *Daily Telegraph*, 19th April 1988.

[118] *Daily Telegraph*, 2nd July 1988.

[119] *South London Press*, 8th Nov. 1977.

[120] *Guardian*, 24th May 1996.

[121] *Guardian*, 30th July 1991.

[122] *The Express*, 3rd Dec. 1997.

[123] *Daily Record*, 24th Aug. 1996.

[124] *Sunday Times*, 15th June 1997.

[125] *Belfast Telegraph*, 16th March 1998, article by Paul Donovan.

[126] *The Viet Vet Survival Guide*, Ballantine Books, New York 1985.

[127] *Home From the War – Vietnam Veterans neither Victims or Executioners*, by Robert Jay Lifton, Beacon Press Boston 1992.

[128] *The Psychologist*, August 1997.

[129] *Falling Out – A Research Study of Homeless Ex-service People*, by Geoffrey Randall and Susan Brown, CRISIS 1994.

[130] *Ibid*.

[131] *Ibid*.

[132] *Guardian*, 4th Nov. 1992, 'The mind as combat zone', by Martin Collins.

[133] *Mail on Sunday Magazine*, 15th Jan. 1995, article on soldiers and PTSD by Jean Rafferty.

[134] *Observer Life*, interview by Andrew Billen, 10th March 1996.

[135] *Observer Magazine*, 10th June 1990, detailed five page article by Peter Nasmyth.

[136] *The Viet Vet Survival Guide*, Ballantine Books, New York 1985.

[137] 'Their Country's Reward', by Jimmy Johnson, unpublished.

[138] *Independent On Sunday*, 7th June 1998, 'Coming Home', by John Davison.

Shoplifter jailed for killing

SHOPLIFTER Andrew Bray was today jailed for five years for killing a schoolboy supermarket worker who chased him.

Slimly built 17-year-old Jonathan Roberts died 90 minutes after ex-Gulf War veteran Bray, 25, kicked and punched him unconscious in a car park at the Somerfield Supermarket in Plymouth.

The athletic part-time shelf stacker died from inhaling his own vomit after a confrontation with Bray, who had left the store pushing a trolley loaded with goods he had not paid for.

Former soldier Bray, from Lipson, Plymouth, had pleaded not guilty at Plymouth Crown Court to murdering Jonathan

THE PEOPLE, September 2, 1990

Love crazy guardsman hijacks car at gunpoint

LOVESICK soldier hijacked a car at gunpoint early yesterday and set off on a 200-mile dash to his girlfriend.

The 22-year-old Grenadier Guardsman, in full combat gear and with camouflage paint smeared on his face, drove at Surrey, Jast

...ion from asking away a couple from their Tudor Rose pub.

Then he headed north towards Cheshire, where his family and girlfriend

Jail for soldier shot after taking rifle

AN armed soldier who escaped from an Army guard room and was shot as he... children playing nearby was jailed for four years yesterday.

Pte Wayne Lawn, 21, who was being held after going absent, had seized a loaded SA80 automatic rifle and was threatening to kill other soldiers at Catterick Camp, North Yorkshire, Teesside Crown Court was told.

Lawn ignored three orders to drop the gun and was hit in the chest when police fired 18 rounds, William Lowe, prosecuting,

Lawn, of the Duke of Own Regiment... admitted... and ammunition... threat to kill an... arm to escape.

Mr Lowe said the... vate had overpowered... try at knifepoint to... with the weapon. Lawn... intensive care for thre... after the shooting.

Earlier he had told... prisoner at Bourlon B... Catterick that he would... to blow somebody aw... said Mr Lowe.

Mr Lowe added:... were children playin... nearby gardens of... ried quarters. A sol... had armed himself... decision, the... rightly, that he... but to discharge...

The soldier... Lawn in the... Military Ho...

Top-level praise saves attacker from prison

DERBYSHIRE TIMES 15 APRIL 1994

AN EX-SOLDIER who attacked his girlfriend after a row in a Chesterfield nightclub escaped jail because he is wanted back in the forces.

The former Commanding Officer of ex-private Matthew Redman wrote to Court praising Redman's record and asking him t... Redman pleaded guilty... after a night... Cheryl... ...he ran...

GUARDIAN 10/7/91

Ex-paratrooper stabbed lovers

...R paratrooper was... five years at the... ...terday for a bayo... ...on his ex-girlfriend... ...r lover as they were in...

...el Lamb, aged 31, was... d of causing grievous... rm, with intent, to ac... ...lie Minskoff, 23, and... ...l Cormack, 24.

...was told how Mr... ...ched the couple... ...uise Miss Minskoff's... at in the early... ...ary 8. Police... ...er, arrived to... ...inskoff bleeding

...amb said he had not in... ...ed to harm the couple, but... ...onsidered using the bayo... ...e his own life.

PARA STAMPS ON BOY'S HEAD AFTER BAG MIX-UP

By CARL JOHNSTON

A BOY of 14 on a school outing was beaten to a pulp by a soldier on a crowded railway platform — because he picked up the wrong bag.

Policeman's son Jamie McIlloy was left unconscious after the 19-year-old off-duty paratrooper punched and kicked him then stamped on his head with both feet.

Last night, dad Keith was keeping a bedside vigil, as doctors feared the boy may suffer permanent brain damage.

Jamie and two pals had been given permission by teachers to wander off and ring their parents.

But as Jamie left the phone booth he picked up a leather holdall identical to his own.

He realised his mistake and put it down but the squaddie, who was watching from another booth, charged at him.

He GRABBED Jamie around the neck, held him in an arm lock and repeatedly punched his head and face.

Bleeding

As the youngster fell into a pool of blood, the soldier STAMPED on his head and kicked his face before picking up his bag and walking away.

The thug then wheeled around and KICKED Jamie twice in the head, picked him up, whispered into his ear and dropped him again.

Last night, Jamie, of Reading, Berks, after visiting a Warrior museum at Eastleigh, near Southampton.

The soldier, who boxes for the Army at Aldershot, Hants, was going home on leave. He has been charged with grievous bodily harm and freed on police bail.

trains at Reading, Berk.,

SENTRY SHOOTS HIMSELF

GIRLFRIEND trouble led an Army corporal to shoot himself in the stomach while on sentry duty early yesterday.

But he cheated death when the bullet penetrated his stomach and came out of his back.

Last night the 21-year-old was "satisfactory" in hospital in Salisbury

Police said the rifleman, a member of the 14th Field Regiment at Larkhill Barracks, near Amesbury, Wilts, blasted himself with his own weapon because he was "in distress over a girlfriend," according to a note he left.

Soldier jailed for seven years for river bank rape

THE HERALD 21 May 1993

SOLDIER Allan Ritchie was jailed for seven years yesterday for raping a nursery nurse.

The attack, which the Judge heard had devastated the teenager's life, happened on a picturesque river bank in Perthshire, the High Court at Kirkcaldy was told yesterday.

Lord Morton was also told that the young woman, who was on holiday at the family...

...Birnam, he assaulted the 18-year-old, pulled and pushed her on to a bench, struggled with her, lay on top of her, forcibly removed items of her clothing, and attempted to rape her.

He further admitted a similar assault during which he punched her on the face rendering her unconscious, punching her repeatedly on the head and face, butt...

...and "done a runner" but claimed she had been willing to have intercourse with him.

Defence advocate Alan Turnbull, said Ritchie, who had been a soldier since he was 18, had never been in trouble before.

"A culmination of lack of sleep and drunkenness on his part caused him to...

Squaddie's tank joyride

...SOLDIER was being quizzed by police yesterday... ...joyride in a 30-ton ARMOURED CAR.

...Darren, 21, was chased by police... ...went AWOL in a Warrior personal carrier from... ...Lulworth Army camp, Dorset. He... ...an hour later, near the village of... ...20mph but it could have caused a lot of damage.

A police spokesman said: "It was only doing 15 to

... last night another soldier ... is a novel set in West Belfast. It tells the stories of two young people, Billy, a Scottish soldier, and Sorcha, a republican, caught up in the dramatic early years of the 'troubles'.

When British soldiers were first ordered onto the streets of Derry and Belfast in 1969 they were welcomed by many nationalists as protectors against loyalist pogroms. Within two years the army and the nationalist community were locked into a bitter war.

... last night another soldier ... is set amid real events and provides a realistic view, from both sides of the barricades, of ordinary people caught up in a conflict which is not of their own making.

WHAT THE CRITICS HAD TO SAY

'An illuminating account.'
Sandra Barwick – *Independent*

'It is a simple tale, told with a terrible clarity ...
Renwick is a master of dialogue ... (he creates) an
extraordinarily faithful view of a single side of the
North's anguish.'
Fergus Pyle – *Irish Times*

'Renwick writes simply, but very well indeed. He
creates atmosphere and suspense; the way he
depicts incidents can bring tears to the eyes.'
Geoffrey Bell – *London-Irish News*

'Though there is violent death there is compassion
too – and all of the time a searching for truth.'
Irish Post

**Cover price £3.95 paperback, 192 pages, illustrated,
ISBN O 9512839 1 X**
Trade distribution by Turnaround Distribution,
Available by post from Barbed Wire, PO Box 958,
London W14 OJF for £5 (p&p inclusive for the UK and
Ireland – other countries add £1). Make cheques
payable to Barbed Wire (because of the high cost of
changing foreign cheques, we can only accept payment
in sterling).

A Barbed Wire Book

Barbed Wire is a voluntary group which
aims to help the cause of truth and peace
in Ireland by highlighting the hidden
issues from nearly three decades of
conflict. Formed in 1998, the group is
independent, self-funded and non-profit-
making.